THE **HARDER I**
FIGHT THE **MORE**
I LOVE
YOU

THE HARDER I FIGHT THE MORE I LOVE YOU

A MEMOIR

NEKO CASE

GRAND CENTRAL

New York Boston

Copyright © 2025 by Neko Case

Cover design and photo by Neko Case.
Cover copyright © 2025 by Hachette Book Group, Inc.

Grand Central Publishing
Hachette Book Group
1290 Avenue of the Americas, New York, NY 10104
grandcentralpublishing.com
@grandcentralpub

First Edition: January 2025

Grand Central Publishing is a division of Hachette Book Group, Inc. The Grand Central Publishing name and logo is a registered trademark of Hachette Book Group, Inc.

The publisher is not responsible for websites (or their content) that are not owned by the publisher.

The Hachette Speakers Bureau provides a wide range of authors for speaking events. To find out more, go to hachettespeakersbureau.com or email HachetteSpeakers@hbgusa.com.

Grand Central Publishing books may be purchased in bulk for business, educational, or promotional use. For information, please contact your local bookseller or the Hachette Book Group Special Markets Department at special.markets@hbgusa.com.

Print book interior design by Marie Mundaca

Library of Congress Cataloging-in-Publication Data has been applied for.

ISBNs: 978-1-5387-1050-0 (hardcover), 978-1-5387-1052-4 (ebook), 978-1-5387-7315-4 (BN.com signed edition), 978-1-5387-7316-1 (signed edition)

Printed in the United States of America

LSC-C

Printing 1, 2024

For Tara and the Fortinis

Contents

Contents

Prologue

Let the show begin! I caw "Hello!" to the audience and the bass player counts in the song, because that's not one of my strong suits. Within the first few words I feel a little rage heat up in my chest. The sound isn't yet graspable; I'm flashing with embarrassment like an electric eel (don't let them see that, idiot!!) and I don't quite recognize myself. I want to slap away the feeling, so I shift my legs slightly, trying to take my mind off the beginnings of a yeast infection from the constant heat and a shitty, sugary diet of bread, cola, and french fries. The wave of small rage breaks over me and I press on. I feel a little more confident as the chorus arrives and my bandmates lock in.

My job at that moment is to conjure a small dust devil of unreality around us, to pull it up out of a sticky, shiny carpet and flappy, beer-soaked speaker cones. I have to make it out of words and sounds and looks. Dirty glitter, memories, lust, desire, regret. I have to pretend I'm wise about love. I have to make the twenty-two people including the bartender and my bandmates think this is real, too. Despite my self-consciousness about the cheap, off-color concealer spackling the zits around my mouth, my filthy clingy clothes lodged in parts of my forever chubby midsection, my complete lack of style, I continue to play and try to make myself believe it. There's absolutely no reason on paper that I should feel brave enough to do this, but I can't help it.

"I can't help it" is a good stopgap answer to most questions about pursuing a creative life, the only one that makes sense when you don't have the time or wherewithal to explain it, or if you just don't think it's anyone else's business. You can get to the "why" some other time. Making music is a soft rebellion in a world that's always at your shoulder asking, "What makes you think you're so important that someone should listen to you?" It's a question that can get leveled at you in a hundred different ways, but its intent is always the same: to defeat you before you even try. I grew up believing I was nothing, and sometimes my own insignificance wracked me with pain. But luckily, somewhere down the line, I came to realize that if I'm nothing, and I have nothing, what is the real risk of putting myself out there? If I'm so forgettable, my humiliation will just be a short weather event. A needly little rain shower. I can live with that. There are way worse things to be remembered as.

There are no grounding, solid answers, just laughter. The nightly conjuring of the luminous dust devil is its own reward. The bonds with the other people involved are the greater reward, not that being "rewarded" is the goal. Living the small rebellion against nothingness and corruption is what helps you exist at all in such a divided country where the patriotic "we" means rich white men. The rule makers don't want us to know each other in real life, they want us to know "of" each other only, and fearfully at that; you'll see it on the nightly news in every region. Meeting, in person, as many people as possible is what smashes the illusion that we have no connection with "us" beyond some racist anthems and the pledge of allegiance.

I love a stranger and a new city, and I want to know their stories. They are so powerful in their possibilities. Are they a friend? A game changer, a storm, catalyst, true love, future bandmate, major influence, will they become a guiding coordinate? How many of these people you meet and truly connect with rests on your level of engagement. It's bigger or smaller depending on your mind: if you're depressed or curious or exhausted. There are stretches of time that add up to literal years that I don't remember, just because I was so sad. I mourn those years. The happiness of the soft rebellion, however, holds those years in its arms and hums and sways. It is a real and loving home.

As the soft rebellion gains speed, I feel my whole being stuffed up inside my mouth. I wonder, oh so fleetingly, how I got here. It's a forbidden question; the mere thinking of it could open a trapdoor beneath my feet, and if I don't wipe it away quick enough I'll fall through. It's a rabbit-hole vacuum and I swat the question from my mind. But it's too late. I see a kid running down the grayest street possible. At first she looks gray, too. But then I see the embers of rage flying off her. She has rivulets of fur trickling out of her sleeves and down the back of her neck, a stray's three-beat gait. She is not even a she at all, just an animal running, as hard as it can, panting, out of breath.

THE HARDER I FIGHT THE MORE I LOVE YOU

Chapter 1

If a Doe and a Tree Had a Baby

Here's something about me: I have never seen a ghost. That probably doesn't seem odd, but no one wants to see one more than I do. I guess I just want it too badly—my eagerness is repellent to them. I represent no thrill, I'm too easy.

I have never seen a ghost, but I have been haunted.

It was by a recurring dream I had as a little kid. In it, I am about four or five, shopping downtown with my mother, eye level with shopping bags and strollers and folded umbrellas. I remember Dolly Parton's face looking back at me from the cover of her album in the window of the Payless store. She wore denim and a bandanna on her head like my mom did sometimes, and big hoop earrings, too. Her smile looked so warm and entrancing. I think that part was based on real memory. We were on Holly Street. I had walked it a million times, heading to the Bon Marché, where my mom worked waiting tables in the department store's café. I sometimes went with my dad to pick her up after her shift, and often she'd let me get a box of chewy toffee caramel from Scotland. There were beautiful embossed thistles in varying colors on the thick wrappers to denote the flavor: salted, lavender, chocolate, and so on. The individual candies were folded inside delicate tissue.

In the dream there were no toffees. No stopping at the café. The day was gray. But the days were always, always gray in Bellingham, Washington. Even the gum on the sidewalk was gray. My mother stopped me to look through some barrel-shaped sales bins, and my craning gaze wandered through the legs of the shuffling crowd of weekend shoppers. To my left was a vending machine. I was drawn to the round, fake-fruit jelly candy. The colors throbbed and my eyes locked onto them, like a high-powered microscope with a tractor beam. I could see the rectangular specks of sugar getting bigger, smothering every centimeter of the glowing candy discs. I thought about how when you'd bite into one of the candies it would feel like a dead cartoon character's tongue, like you were a shark taking a perfect crescent-shaped bite out of a swollen gray whale carcass. The veins on the bottom of my own tongue ached sympathetically at the thought. I could taste it: fluorescent orange and lemon and lime, and stale blood.

"Momma?" I said.

But she was gone. She had just been standing here. She couldn't be far. I frantically tried to lock onto some fleeting, familiar part of her before she disappeared completely. I saw the back of her long, nut-brown hair flash like a bronze goldfish as it disappeared underwater ahead.

"Momma!"

She got smaller. I got louder.

I shrieked: "MOMMA! WAIT FOR ME!"

I yelled so hard I lost control of my body and squeezed a bit of pee into my underwear. *I can't cry! Everyone will know!* I shook and sobbed, but without tears. It physically hurt. I was panicking now, and I ran forward. The crowd didn't even notice me and pressed in, en masse. Strangers' coats—camel, gray, and powder blue—choked my mouth and nose, blocking my way. When the coats cleared, my mom was gone.

This is how a ghost might disappear, I guess, but what did that make my mom? A ghost or a charged space left by a theft?

This is how my story starts; with a clichéd and prophetic recurring dream. A short time later, in real life, my mother *would* disappear, but in a way far more complicated and destructive, a stunt so bizarre I'm reluctant to even tell it as it's completely unbelievable. Looking back, my childhood seems like a movie, as though it all happened to someone else. Until I see my own face in a photograph or reflected in a window. I look just like her, which makes me wish I looked like *anyone else.*

The dream seems more real than my memories, but I think that's just because it makes more sense than how she really disappeared.

My parents were the typical cautionary tale of two teens who have sex for the first time ever, in a car (of course!), and get pregnant by accident. They both went to Lynden High School, in a little town in western Washington State, and had only been dating a short time. They were seventeen and eighteen and poor as empty acorns. It was the tail end of the Vietnam War, that cataclysm that held everyone's attention in a nauseating chokehold. So my dad joined the air force, and he and my mom got married. "That's just what you did." My mom later said my dad had written her a poem, while my dad said that my mom had used him to get away from her family. "Trapped me" were, I believe, his exact words. He'd also later claim, "I didn't even know she was pregnant," a story that doesn't hold water as there's a photo of the two of them drinking Cokes together when she was about four months along. Needless to say, these two young people had no business being together and even less business forcing a human soul into this world. They would not have more children together, and they would *not* stay married more than a handful of years. Luckily, my dad wasn't sent to Vietnam; he served at Fort Belvoir, outside Alexandria, Virginia. Unluckily, he and my mom had to hang out with each other. So there I was, with no siblings and a pair of stressed and uninterested parents who didn't actually like each other: a child of children.

It's not a surprise that my first memory is one of neglect—and, given everything that would come later, that I mistook that neglect for beauty. It starts with a near drowning, and all the other details I remember of that time flow out of it, like ink spreading in water. I was very, very little, just walking with any confidence. I was wearing white patent leather Mary Janes and walking along the sidewalk outside the apartment building where we lived, past the edge of the pool where people were swimming.

I moved toward the pool with intent. I stepped off the edge as I had seen the other people do. I went down fast and then slow. I opened my eyes. The sunlight danced across the bottom of the aqua blue in a loose, billowing net. The swimmers' legs moved in slow motion, the magnificent colors of their swimsuits fluorescent with acid saturation. I was flying under the surface, too small to panic; I didn't breathe in and choke. I think my body knew what to do, even though I'd only ever been in kiddy pools, but before I could find out, my dad's legs appeared, Jesus sandals and all, and I was out of the water in a flash.

I was drowning in flight under the surface of the water, and then being lifted out of it and alive.

When my dad got out of the air force, his parents came to pick us up. He was stationed at Cape Canaveral in Florida by then, and my Grandpa and Gramma Case arrived in a bright-yellow school bus from the Lynden School District, and we drove back to Washington in a long diagonal swipe west. My parents got a little trailer somewhere just outside Bellingham for us to live in. My dad started trade school to become a draftsman, and my mom got a job at a plant nursery.

In Florida, there had been Cocoa Beach and the crabs that moved sideways in groups across the sand, a rippling texture, little magicians of harmless danger, their black eyes atop long stalks like cartoon exclamation points. They were part translucent and part a sunny, lemony, pale yellow, as fast as lightning and able to deliver a nasty pinch. Now, in Washington, everything was shadow colored, and the cold heavy dampness in the air was new but somehow easier to breathe. There were ferns outside the trailer with little rusty-brown velvet tracks like vampire bites on the undersides of their leaves, and I would lie on the ground under the slate sky and pet the soft dots for hours.

Often, we'd drive over to see my mom's mom, my Gramma Mary Ann. She lived in Lynden in a tiny, shabby house. I loved going there. There would be music playing, and brown coffee jumping around in the glass cap of the aluminum percolator on the stove. My gramma had dark curly hair and wore horn-rimmed glasses, and whenever I was with her it seemed like she was always smiling and making pleased noises over me. My mom's little sister, Debbie, just a few years younger than her, was still in high school. She had smooth, pretty ice-cream-blond hair, and was funny and affectionate. I never asked where my grandfather was—it was just understood he wasn't around.

Other weekends, we'd go visit my dad's parents, Gramma and Grandpa Case. They also lived in Lynden, in a low, sprawling single-story house that my dad had helped my grandfather build. The house had green shag carpet that looked like grass and a natural stone fireplace hearth that my cousins and I would play cars and farm animals on, and a little yellow spare room with two twin beds that we cousins got to sleep in.

My Case grandparents, Claude and Lucille, were originally from Alma, Oklahoma. Grandpa Claude had been a thirty-second-degree Mason and superintendent of schools in Lynden (hence the school bus he and my gramma had picked us up in in Florida). But by the time I knew him he lived mostly in a green and yellow plaid recliner and rarely got up. I had no idea he was riddled with cancer and heart disease from a lifetime of smoking and doing god knows what else serving in the Korean War. He was rather gray and see-through and had liver spots across his scalp.

My Gramma Lucille was thin and quick as a bird. She was an upstanding Methodist and a leading member of the Eastern Star, the women's division of the Freemasons who were "allowed" to do charity work. She had a ton of friends, a kind woman who was also no bullshit. She didn't sugarcoat stuff, even for children. She *loved* being married and being a homemaker; she cooked, cleaned, sewed all the family's clothes, kept a magnificent garden, canned produce—the whole works—but she also managed to give me incredibly feminist advice sometimes. For example, she always told me not to worry about getting married unless I really wanted to. She and my granddad had married late for the time, in their mid-thirties, and for love. Everyone, she told me, had thought she was silly for waiting, but she knew. "Young ladies," she would say, "can be whatever they want to be." But later she would also tell me I "walked like a hussy," which I found endlessly funny, and that I needed to brush my hair, a comment she'd keep making for the next thirty years.

She was a no-nonsense woman, but she had a real soft spot

for my mom, her daughter-in-law. "That sweet girl," she called her, even later, after everything busted up.

My dad was like a tree, handsome, six feet tall, with brown curls and very dark brown eyes. Slim, with a slight belly and no butt, he was a quiet, even timid guy, and wore a beard and mustache to hide behind, and often a cowboy hat. At twenty-one, his life hadn't yet gone completely off the rails.

In those days he and my mom had a light green station wagon. It looked like a nauseous basking shark. One afternoon, he and I were driving along to pick her up at Marvin Gardens, the nursery where she was working. It was located a good way outside Bellingham proper, on twisty Chuckanut Drive. It was a gorgeous early-summer day, the shade of the trees bending over the road. Here lived all the shades of green there are, flickering and dancing in the sun. There was some new lovely vista around every corner and every now and again a little meadow would come into view. My eyes ached to take it all in. Suddenly my dad began to slow the car.

"Look over there!" he whispered. He pointed to a group of deer browsing just off the road in a shady little glen. He pulled the car over on a straightaway so we could observe them.

He gave me the "Shhhhh, c'mon!" signal with his index finger and a sideways twitch of his head. We quietly got out of the car, and I tiptoed around to his side. Since the grass in the meadow was taller than me, he hoisted me silently up onto his shoulders. To my surprise he slowly crossed the road and began to walk toward the deer. The smell of sun-warmed grass filled the air. There were grasping ferns and impossible magenta foxgloves with burgundy-spotted throats reaching up to me like I was floating over them in a palanquin. It's like they wanted to touch the royal cuffs of my jeans. I held my breath as we got closer to the deer. There were five or so and at least two spotted babies. My dad and I communicated by ESP that this was unbelievable magic and that we were both freaking out. How was this even *possible*?! Why weren't they running away?!

Golden hour was a ways off, and the deer contrasted with the rich, verdant glow of the meadow; their cinnamon syrup colors even looked as if they tasted sweet. Their tails and ears flicked lazily, and they seemed to take no notice of us. We were among them now. Every now and again an adult would lift her head, blinking her impossibly long lashes and rotating her lower jaw almost mechanically as she chewed. She would look about, then go back to grazing, shaking off a fly or two with her surprisingly long tail.

Dad and I were barely breathing. I was close to one of the fawns now. My heart broke as I noticed the spots set into its gold coat, the color of clotted cream daubed by some graceful brush into a loose, intermittent pattern on its side. The movements of the deer were so fluid it took my breath away. If I had seen them break and run that day my life would have fled out of my chest after them, but they let me live, gentle creatures that they are.

My family was already unhappy, and we were only going to get unhappier. Our miserableness enacted itself as a series of moves from one tiny old house to another, our path around Bellingham like the cracked jagged part of a water-damaged ceiling that's eventually going to cave. But all the time something about this day remained knit into me, reinforcing my bones. I didn't yet have words for it, and I wouldn't for many years, but it was a feeling like nature and I shared a secret.

Chapter 2

I Make Horses Appear

I was fascinated by fairy tales and old folktales back then, attracted to how they could be delicate and brutal and funny all at the same time. An old Grimms' one especially enchanted me. It was about a mother goat who leaves her seven children for the day as she goes off to the forest to look for food. While she's gone a wolf comes to the door, and even though she's warned her children not to open the door, they do. The wolf eats them all. But when the goat mother returns she doesn't blink an eye. She slices open the wolf, pulls out all her children, stuffs the wolf's belly full of logs, and sews him back up. Later, when the wolf drinks from the river, the weight of the logs makes him topple over into the water and drown. All of this made deep sense to me—it held some electric truth. The landscape of the story, with its forests and its shadows, its powerful goat mother and the wolf knocking at the door, seemed as real to me as our tiny house with the cars going by outside. It was bristling fur slicked backward with rational blood.

My mother was young and beautiful, even more vivid and bright than any storybook illustration. She often wore a bandanna over her hair, I guess because it was the seventies and lots of ladies did. She was also, in retrospect, not far enough removed from being an immigrant farmer's daughter to wear it as strictly a fashion choice. It was her ancient costume; she was a little *zhenshina* born in the middle of a bunch of siblings, who spent her childhood picking rocks out of fields and milking cows and popping the bot fly larvae out of the Holsteins' backs. The scarf over her hair was a confirmation of her genetic birthright. And she radiated something when she wore it that I was drawn to.

It was a soft summer day, and I was about to start kindergarten. My mother had left her job at the Marvin Gardens nursery by then and begun working at the café in the Bon Marché. She was popular with the customers—she was appealing, with her green eyes and long brown hair, and had a way of making herself agreeable to people. She could seem malleable and soft, with a pretty way of smiling that showed all her pretty teeth. We were getting ready to walk to the school for an orientation. I was getting dressed and I decided I wanted to wear a bandanna over my hair, too. It was an occasion, and I wanted to look like her. I stood on the closed toilet lid, looked in the mirror, and tried to get the bandanna just right. My mother popped her head in and scolded me to stop looking at myself.

"You're going to become vain," she said.

She stared at me, her eyes so flat. The pretty her was there, but something insidious had flared out from her being.

I froze, startled to be caught doing something wrong that I had no idea was wrong. Something tumbled inside me. I felt a twinge of numbness in my joints and my stomach sank as I flushed with embarrassment. I knew this woman—not my mother, but another her I recognized. She had flared out at me this way before. The first time I was at that tail end of being a toddler, squirming a bit as my mom was trying to get my feet into tights. One second things were normal, the next her head was reared back and her teeth bared, and with flat, tepid eyes she snapped at me...seemingly animated from something outside her body, a bigger, monstrous place. She said something about not wanting to be there and that if I didn't exist she would be free. She had never spoken to me like that before, but then again she wasn't really talking *to* me. It was more like a malevolent gas of some unhinged spirit hissed through her teeth. I was terrified. She flared and faded in front of my eyes.

Now this *other* her was here again, as she said, "You're going to become vain." It was a simple statement, but it was enough to tell me that her love, all love, was not unconditional. She was not like dogs and cats and grass and the sky. I would come to realize she was not my world, just an actor in it, free to come and go as the storms moved her. She was not a guarantee.

Embarrassment, then shame shot through me, filling in like choking sand. I looked from the mirror down at the white, chipped enamel of the sink. I couldn't believe how careless I had been. I had no idea that could happen! I now know that when I was looking in the mirror, I was trying to see her in me. I wasn't looking for my own flatterable "beauty." I was just looking for her. But from her expression I deduced that vanity must be the worst sin on earth. After that, I went out of my way not to call attention to myself. That incident was always at the ready in my mind, and it influenced a lot of things I would go on to do as a kid and things I did even into my late forties and probably still do now.

That morning, I kept the navy-blue bandanna on simply to hide under.

Later, my mother would tell me a story about a time at Bon Marché when she'd "accidentally" spilled coffee in the lap of a customer who'd been abusive to her. That anecdote holds some sort of key to her—the girl with the smile like a shield, thinking her own private thoughts behind it, some of them angry and violent. Still, I reached for her, more than I ever did my father. She was the country I was from, and I worshiped her. She was the sun.

There is a scene in the Grimms' fairy tale where the wolf, trying to get inside, pretends to be the children's mother. It talks to them in her sweet voice. The children have been warned. They know better! And still they can't seem to help it—hearing their mother's voice, they open the door.

Other times my mom might correct me, be impatient, even yell, but that sort of thing never bothered me. That was, I recognized, just a parent being a parent. Those two flares of the other her were something entirely different. At some level, below words or even thought, I absorbed that there was something shameful about me that kept her love for me from being definite. And so I would contort myself into all sorts of shapes to try to please her. In my attempts to make her love for me concrete, I tried to be less wiggly and willful, to make myself sweet and compliant. Almost an invisible child. And I might have melted myself out of existence if a bit of magic hadn't happened.

It was morning, and I was standing on the porch outside our house. You could see the sign for KFC and smell chicken, too. I was thinking about horses, as I always was then. It was like I had shuddered into being with the idea of horses already in my system. I was so in love with horses I thought about them all the time. *All* the time. There had been a gorgeous plastic bay stallion at my nursery school, and I would ride him for hours, stimming away to the sounds of the springs as we galloped around the world. Now, I gazed at the outbuildings of our neighbors' houses, noticing how they looked somehow agricultural, like feed shacks. They may have been at one time, but my mind made them all into stables, every single garage and gardening shed on the street.

I suddenly felt very frustrated. *Why was it so hard to be near them?! Why couldn't we just move to the country!?* The tide of disappointment reached its zenith right behind my eyes, then began to drain, back out toward the unseeable edge of my invisible universe. I softened a little and thought, *OK! I am going to see a horse right…NOW!*

So I clench-focused as hard as I could, like a toad-sized Olympic Kegeling wizard: *Rrrrrrrrrr!* I slammed my eyelids open and lo and behold, not one, but TWO horses came walking down the alley on the opposite side of the street toward me! Complete with the gorgeous sound of their hard feet hitting the ground like music. Their bodies together were a rhythm section, and the women on their backs dancers of special beauty and privilege. HOLY SHIT! I had actually DONE IT. I had made horses appear!!! I was paralyzed with awe and disbelief.

The horse closest to me was a gray, and the other was a sorrel. They were being ridden by two young women. What are the odds? We lived in a city. How was this possible if I hadn't *made* it happen? I felt satisfaction flood through me. In that moment there was nothing left to wish for, it was a real arrival to a real place that was my individual personhood, if only for a few minutes. After you've seen that person, you can't unsee them, even if they go absent for years at a time. You might even try to erase this self, and still it will come flashing back before you. At fifty-two years old, I can still see the horses clear as day.

I was small and grubby, and that was okay because every kid I played with was small and grubby, too. We were all scrappers, all of us from families with no money. Nobody's pants were long enough. My first friend, a girl named Dundee, and I fist-fought on her lawn, then made up and played some more. The days went by in that way of childhood, where the borders of what's ordinary and what's strange, what's a fairy tale and what's life are blurred. The lines between animals and humans likewise were gorgeously loose. The tiny crabs that had skittered across the beach, the deer in the woods, they were as intriguing to me as Dundee was. At night I would dream of my mother going missing, and wake up having pissed the bed, but I also was happy in my way.

One day my parents came home with a puppy, a little wiry white thing, no bigger than a pair of bundle-folded gym socks, unsure and wiggling up the steps. She was the color of a vanilla milkshake. I would get to name her. There was a singer I loved to listen to on the CBC, Buffy Sainte-Marie. She had a version of "Cripple Creek" that was just her and a jaw harp, which held me fixated in front of the radio every time it came on. Her voice was the sonic equivalent of watching the coffee leaping and bubbling into the clear glass knob of the percolator at Gramma Mary Ann's house. It seemed right that this wondrous creature would have her name, so "Buffy" it was. I got down on the floor in the living room and she jumped onto my lap, wiggling like she had an Evinrude engine bolted to her back end. I took her in my arms and felt her wiry-soft fur. I felt the tickling of her little snout snuffling around in my hair until she found my earlobe and gnawed it with her needly little puppy teeth. I was as happy in that moment as was humanly possible.

Shortly after Buffy came home, my mom moved out. She got an apartment with her little sister Debbie. At first, I would go over once a week or so to see her. They had an over-lacquered game table with a board on it you could use for chess or checkers, which I thought gave the apartment a pizza parlor feel. The Hall and Oates song "Rich Girl" was out then, and it always seemed to be playing on the radio when I was over, ever shocking for the part where Daryl Hall would sing, "It's a bitch, girl." Listening to music and plunking the checkers around the table, I could forget how much my mom had confused me by leaving, and how she was already starting to flicker like a lightbulb about to go out.

It wasn't great, but, I thought, I could live with it. I mean, what choice did I have?

Chapter 3

The Wake

Then it happened. I told you it would.

I was at my Gramma Lucille's house in Lynden. It was a gray and drizzly day. My dad came to pick me up, and when we got in the car, the windshield wipers slapped away the bouncing rain, changed the scene from a blur of gray curtain to my gramma's geraniums in their concrete planter, their usually happy fluorescent coral faces smearing grotesque through the wipers. My dad turned to me, his usually stoic face clenched. I tensed. He made some strange noises and then said, "Your mommy died."

What?

But then my dad was sobbing, and I felt fear move through me, cold as Novocaine. He never even really talked, let alone cried. I asked if he was sure. I asked what happened. He replied, "Your mommy was very sick." I knew she'd been to the doctor a few times, but this was news to me. I think he said the word "cancer." But if she was so sick, why didn't I know?! Why hadn't I seen more of her? I started to cry in earnest.

My mom had already seemed too far away, like she was Dopplering into a blur. She had started dating Bill, a shorter, stout guy who looked exactly like Teddy Roosevelt or David Crosby, depending on his hair length at the time. He was loud and from western Massachusetts. I liked him—he exuded a warm good-heartedness—but I was very reserved around him, I'm sure, as the more my mom moved away from me, the more wary I became of the other people she wanted to fill her life with. I'd been to his place a couple of times, an upstairs apartment on Iron Street. He was a college student, so the decor was concert posters and records, and a kitchen table made of an industrial wooden spool.

Both my mom and dad had been even more distracted than usual. When they talked, I heard mentions of doctors' appointments, but I hadn't thought much of it. I was mostly consumed with wanting a baton—either blue or silver. We had no money, so I found an old curtain rod at Bill's place and spent hours trying to teach myself tricks in the dirt front yard, blissfully unaware of worry, just liking how strong my arm looked making wide figure-eight twirls with my fake baton.

The highway back to our house from Gramma Lucille's was a straight shot, and my dad and I drove through the rain, both of us quietly crying but immeasurably separate from each other, alone in our sorrow.

Not long after, my Gramma Mary Ann held a wake. Mom had been cremated. It was a sunny day, and the grass in the yard had been recently mowed. Card tables had been set up outside with trays of food. About twenty or thirty people were there. I floated in and out of the house, eating potato chips and carrot sticks and onion dip. Nothing felt real until I saw my aunt Sue coming toward me. She was married to my mom's older brother, and I was crazy about her. A short woman with straight, dark brown hair, she'd wrinkle her nose a little like a rabbit when she laughed or smiled, which she did easily. Today, however, she looked sad as she leaned down to hug me. *I'm sorry,* she said, reaching out her arms. My dad had been like a locked box ever since he'd told me the news, and that had kept me like a locked box, too. Now, something broke open inside. As Sue hugged me, I began to cry a little but was embarrassed, so I wiped my tears and nose on my sleeve.

Silently, my dad and I returned home. We were living in a house on Grant Street, and from the moment we had moved in, one of my biggest fears about the house was my bedroom window, which looked out onto the backyard and the *very* hefty laundry line held up by two *thick*, tree-sized poles. Each pole had another heavy piece of wood fastened across it to hold two parallel clotheslines, which made them look like two giant crosses. In my mind, crosses equaled graves. At night, a streetlight across the alley would come on and backlight them dramatically. Lying in my bed, I'd be frozen in terror, staring out at them. But Buffy would snuggle close, and I'd make a barrier of stuffed animals around us. I'd level out my heartbeat by syncing it with hers, and I would fall asleep. The night after my mom's wake, the giant, backlit crosses loomed larger than ever, and even Buffy's steady heartbeat couldn't calm me.

The days wore on, a combination of disbelief and darkness. I went back to school, but I was so distracted I just floated through, my teacher's voice never reaching me. My life became a subterranean furrow; I could see light but it never translated to warmth. My dad didn't speak anymore, just a grunt now and then. When I came home the house was empty except for Buffy, who was mercifully oblivious to my sorrow. When my dad arrived home from work around five or six there'd be no talk of dinner. I'd make a plate of cheese and crackers or eat a couple of slices of bread out of the bag as we sat watching reruns. He'd smoke weed out of a bong and stare straight ahead, glassy eyed, at some television show or listen to *Blood on the Tracks*. He played it over and over and over. Even in second grade I felt its staggering sadness. I was a drip of paint dropped onto a foundation on the shady side between two worlds, where the sun barely touches. I was drying slowly. I went to bed every night at nine. I didn't even bother trying to bargain an extra ten minutes here and there anymore, like all kids do. We were two zombies rattling through the house. When I went out into the world, everything looked like a prison hallway from TV, gray and riveted with too-large bolts: the inside of the school bus, the classroom corridors, my walk home under the I-5 overpass.

Summer came and my dad bought a dilapidated fifties sky-blue Dodge truck. He was good with his hands, and I guess fixing up the truck was a distraction. But where my seat should be, as the rightful passenger, was a disturbing foot-wide hole that looked straight down to the road. When I asked about it, my dad simply threw down a piece of plywood, not even securing it. I sat on the floor with no seat belt or anything to hang on to, noticing how little he seemed to care that I might fall through.

When school started again, they sent me to the school counselor, Mrs. Saddlebrook. She wanted to know why I was so quiet. I was dumbfounded by the question. Had she never visited a fucking classroom? The teacher's every fifth sentence was "Quiet please," "Settle down," or "Please close your mouths and LISTEN!" I was a mild, rule-obeying child, my inner malcontent not yet fully awake, so I DID WHAT THEY SAID! The counselor let me go after twenty minutes. When my dad got home from work I mentioned it to him. I wasn't expecting a reply—I only talked *at* him these days, and even then not very much—but he immediately focused, with a frightening, laser-like intensity. "What did you say? Who was it?"

The next day when he came home, he told me he had been to my school and told them they were *never* to do that again or there would be *very* serious consequences, and he wasn't talking about a lawsuit. He told me to never go with anyone if they didn't have his permission. I thought it so strange that a person who barely acknowledged me would have such a strong reaction. Was I kind of like his "property"? The school didn't send me to the counselor's office again.

Nights throughout this time were especially hard. I missed my mom so bad that sometimes I would take out the homemade makeup bag that she had left behind, cantaloupe orange with white polka dots, unbutton the one large white button, and put my face in and smell her makeup. But it only made me miss her more.

I only remember being comforted once. I was staying over at my cousins' house, sleeping on the top bunk of one of the kids' beds. I couldn't sleep. I missed my mom so much. I cried with longing. I didn't even hear the door crack as my dad's older sister, Aunt Nancy, came in. She stepped onto the mattress frame below and hoisted herself up. "I'm so sorry, honey…I know," she said softly as she smoothed back my hair. "I know." And for a few moments at least I stopped holding my breath.

One day I got a strange box in the mail that had been sent to my Gramma Mary Ann. In it was a very nice, medium-sized, glossy black teddy bear with a pecan-colored snout and paw pads. Also in the box was a royal blue enameled pin of a galloping horse in glorious regalia and a few highly polished stones. They were gorgeous and I remember every single one: a pink one with gray flecks, an amber agate, and a black stone with bits of prehistoric shell embedded in it. No one knew who the presents were from, but they distracted me from my fog for a little bit, I suppose.

Nothing could break the curse, though. I felt like I was on a slow-moving sidewalk, traveling down a long hallway, at the end of which were two gymnasium doors with push bars across the front. I knew that if I passed through them, I would enter a place so much darker than the one I was in now. I was so close to the doors I began to get scared. This vision was in my mind all the time.

One morning I was in the kitchen. My dad came out of his room and, seeing me, he looked surprised, as if he'd forgotten I lived there.

"Oh. I have to make you a lunch, don't I?"

That day we were going on a class field trip to the Vancouver Aquarium, and there would be no cafeteria. My dad sliced up some cheddar cheese and put it in a sandwich baggie. By the time lunch rolled around my cheese was beaded with greasy sweat, curled and cracked around the edges. I remember the look of absolute pity one of the teacher's aides gave me. I dragged that shame around like a wet wool cape.

I was still spending a lot of time with my grandparents, too. When my Grandpa Case had gotten a pacemaker, he let me look at it. It was like he had a baseball sewn under his chest and you could see the stitches embossed on the ball underneath the skin, it was stretched so tight over the tiny machine. At this point he was only wearing pajama pants and hospital gown shirts backward for clothes. I was a little girl, though, and didn't know this meant he was dying. He and my grandmother had a gigantic bed made up of two queen-sized beds. Granddad's half had a motor that helped him sit up, the entire mattress bending into a sort of couch recliner, which I thought was incredibly cool. After he died, shortly after my mom, Gramma kept his half of the huge bed intact. She and I would watch *The Tonight Show* snuggled up together like two little dolls untethered to the deck of the *Kon-Tiki,* adrift somewhere out in the Pacific Ocean, lost and resigned. The prickly, faux-crushed-velvet midnight green of the bedspread, dark and bottomless, itching my legs, Johnny

Carson with his close dome of silver hair rising in front of us like the moon.

At that time in my life I was going to visit Gramma Lucille at least once or twice a month, alternating with Gramma Mary Ann. Sometimes I'd go straight from one to the other for a couple of days. Gramma Mary Ann might pick me up at Gramma Lucille's, and then we'd head to Albertsons to get Fudgsicles. She drove an electric-blue Vega. The interior of the car was a tiny-basket-weave black vinyl, and the buttons on the radio were like fat candy. We'd listen to the oldies country station on the AM dial. Gramma would sing along in the proper "barely louder than under your breath" lady volume. Her voice was sweet, though. It sounded just like the last three Certs candies from the bottom of a purse tasted, like the last candy on earth. She *loved* Marty Robbins, the cloudlike baritone of Jim Reeves, George Strait, and all the "girl singers," like Patsy Cline. I, too, loved when Patsy Cline came on; she held the most fascination for me, along with the funny melody genius Roger Miller. I was lucky both sides of my family loved music. I might not have felt safe enough to even try singing along with the radio if they hadn't been singing along themselves. I would sing with my grandmother and watch the countryside roll by. I knew specifically where every single horse lived in the surrounding fifty square miles.

By then my Gramma Mary Ann had moved to a cute little white house next to a fleet lot for cement mixer trucks. There was a rusty ten-foot chain-link fence guarding these war elephants, all white and gray, but each one having diamond harlequin patterns around the barrels of the mixers in their own individual color. I would stare at them and choose which one I would drive. The magenta won 90 percent of the time. There was also a train track along that fence where I would catch giant grasshoppers and look for railroad spikes.

I was starting to understand that Mary Ann had had a husband once, my mom's dad. Their family name was Shevchenko but had become Hobbs in the United States. I was told that my great-grandparents had emigrated from Russia when my grandfather was just a boy, and that he'd been a twin. I'd met him only once, a couple of years before, when I was young enough to understand that he was my grandfather but not yet old enough to realize that he was my grandmother's ex-husband. He'd been an old man in a chair, with a slight accent and a friendly air. As the adults talked, I had drawn him a picture of a horse. He seemed pleased with it, and as we were leaving, he gave me a fifty-dollar bill. I had never even had twenty dollars, let alone *fifty*! I was elated and confused. "Here you go, Neck-o"—he pronounced my name wrong even though it was exactly the same as the shortened version of *his* name, Nicolas—"since I've never given you anything in your whole life." I hadn't seen him since, and no one ever spoke of him, not my grandmother, not my aunt Debbie, no one. I began to understand that there was violence associated with the very idea of him, and I could start to feel his absence in the sweet yellow living room.

On one of those visits to Gramma Mary Ann, I found a baby rabbit that the cat, Schratzie—a white, sleek empress of a thing with gold eyes that belonged to my aunt Debbie—had abandoned mid-assault. The baby rabbit's tiny, cinnamon-colored ears were plastered to its little neck, and its tiny whiskers buzzed like a Norelco shaver. It was terrified. I sat on the storm door cradling it in my hands as it slowly came to life. I desperately wanted to keep it, but my grandmother gently explained that wild things don't do well in a human house, and its mother was likely missing it, so I placed it tenderly under a bush to wait for its mom. I reluctantly said "goodbye" and went into the house. I knew I wouldn't be able to leave it alone if I stayed outside, and it was getting dark anyway. The next morning it was gone.

One day, walking out of school, I was surprised and relieved to see my dad waiting for me. He never picked me up from school. I had begun to dread the school bus; it was a slow ride to our house and I had to sit alone with my thoughts until I got home and at least had a change of scenery. It was nice to see my dad, even though riding with him would be just as quiet.

When I got into his car, he turned to me and said, "OK, I don't want you to be afraid. Your mommy..." Then he paused, as if unsure how to proceed.

"Your mommy is back, and I don't want you to think she is a ghost."

Despite the shocking news, my first thought was, Are you fucking *kidding* me!? Just how *stupid* do you think I am? I'd know she's not a *ghost*!

I asked, "Mom is *here*?" Hope was wriggling its way up in me. I had been so sad, so colorless. She had been gone for a year and a half, and I was beyond ready to believe *anything* that might change my lot on this earth, and this was the *best* possible scenario; Mom was no longer dead. "Are we going to see her?" I asked, joy, or maybe just heightened relief, building inside of me.

"Yes, we're going right now," he said. "She's at the house."

When we got home, I sprinted into the house and met my mom coming out of my dad's room. It was obvious she had just showered. I ran and hugged her. My eyes canvassed her, greedy for her face, her way of holding herself. Her hair was slightly shorter, but otherwise she looked exactly the same. She told me she had missed me but that she was back now. I opened my mouth to speak. I had so many questions! And yet I sensed that to ask them would be to invite her to disappear all over again, and so I swallowed my questions and buried them deep. That was easy enough—I had so much dumb animal joy rocking through me, I felt myself nearly capsize with it.

Later, it was explained to me that she had had terminal cancer and didn't want me to see her die in a horrible state of deterioration. She faked her death so that no one else would, either. She had traveled to Hawaii, hung out with Buddhists, gone through chemo, and been cured. But she had missed me *so* badly that she had to come home. End of story. The teddy bear and the polished stones had been from her. I didn't fucking care if this all didn't make sense! I forgave her with such desperate haste, I didn't even have time to be mad. The looming doors at the end of the sad hallway that had been haunting me were dead-bolted for good, and I was going to get as far from them as I possibly could.

Life did not return to that sad normal, but something

was still off. My mom had brought a boyfriend with her from Hawaii who looked like a Ken doll. His name was Marty, and he liked to collect exotic fish (because of course he did). The first time my Gramma Mary Ann picked us all up to bring us to her house after my mom returned, I was sitting in the front of her newish, maroon GM sedan. Mom and Marty were in the back seat, French kissing so loudly I turned around and saw the blue veins on the underside of their tongues. They were unfazed at my protest. Gramma said nothing. She was now married to a man named Clyde, a quiet, gentle farmer whom she had known all her life. They lived in a butter-yellow farmhouse out in the Mount Baker hills in a town that no longer exists. When we finally arrived at the house, my mom's brother and sisters and their spouses were there to see Mom for the first time since she "died." I peeked into the living room, then went to the kitchen (I always had to check if there were any Cheetos in the cabinet). From my perch there, I listened to the adults' voices in the other room. Everyone sounded friendly but subdued. There were no exclamations, no weeping. I couldn't understand it! She had returned from the dead! Why weren't people rejoicing? I made my way back into the living room. Aunts and uncles were sitting on the big brown couch, some standing with flimsy paper plates of potato salad. Clyde was in his recliner. It could have been any sort of muted family gathering. Marty sat on the corner of the couch, and I ignored him, going to the table to inspect the food laid out there. There were bowls of onion dip and supermarket Jell-O, the same food that was served at her wake. I dipped chips and swallowed, dutifully, asking nothing.

As it happened, that day would be the last time I saw

Marty, thank god. Soon after, my mom married Bill, her old boyfriend who was now a certified archaeologist. Bill's job took him to lots of different places for digs. Even though I liked Bill, I wondered, did this just mean she'd leave again? I was still so elated my mom was home, but what if I never got to see her? Hadn't she told me that she missed me so much that she'd come back from the dead? She had, but I felt the unfinished math of her disappearance like thunder under the ground.

Chapter 4

Highway to Nespelem

It was spring break, and I was in eastern Washington visiting my mom and Bill. Bill was working at an archaeological dig site on the Columbia River, and he'd brought me along this morning. An archaeological dig is a funny mix. It is delicate, often sacred work when you are handling the bones and belongings of people who lived so long ago, but there is a lot of it, too, that is just the dirty hard labor of moving enormous piles of dirt from one place to another. The ground was staked and churned-up brown, bordered by the green rise of the weeds along the river. It was a good blend of men and women, archaeologists and students on the site—various ages but all shaggy looking and all dressed in dirt-spattered clothes, their bodies burly from the physical requirements of their days. If you didn't know they were archaeologists, you might have mistaken them for hippie lumberjacks.

I had been quivering with excitement since I arrived. My mom and Bill were living in the dig project's camp, which was located about a fifteen-minute drive from the site. The camp consisted of rows and rows of campers, shipping containers, and tents packed on a dirt lot. Bill and my mom lived in one of the shipping containers, a faded yellow one, and that seemed incredibly cool, like living in a roomy lunch box. My mom had hugged me when I arrived, and Bill had showed me the plywood loft where I'd sleep. There was a *very* excited first meeting with our new dog, Bubba, a gray and white malamute Bill had spotted running with a pack of coyotes at the dig site and persuaded to return with him to camp. Bubba was a huge dog with big, soulful eyes, and I loved him immediately, just as I loved the camp with its bustle of people walking by, everyone busy with their work. There was sound, color—everything I missed at home with my dad. And now, this dig.

One of the archaeologists invited me over to the sift table. It was a wooden framed table, about two feet by two feet but tall so that the people at the site wouldn't have to squat to use it. It came up to my breastbone. You spread a shovelful of dirt across the mesh of the top, and then rocked the table to get the dirt to sift through. I felt butterflies jump in my stomach as the dirt was spread for me to sift. I wanted to be taken seriously. I also hoped I would make some astonishing find, like when the dirt had passed through there would be a skull left, or some priceless treasure. I rocked the table with my whole body, making the dirt move through. It wasn't easy, it was like dancing with a small fridge. When the dirt had sifted away, a potsherd lay on top of the mesh.

The next day when I woke up, my mom and Bill were out. I

made my way from our place over to the lab trailers. This was where artifacts pulled from the dig site were deep-cleaned and cataloged, and it was where my mom often worked. I tapped on the door and slid inside. The two lab techs, both youngish women, nodded to me and continued with their work.

I'd seen the lab's two sonic vibration machines at work, and they had entranced me. One was named "Lorraine" and the other "Francine." They were basically metal fish tanks full of water that you would put hard-to-clean fragments of artifacts or bone in, and when you flipped a switch the machines began to buzz like a box of hummingbirds, vibrating so fast that the dirt and fine silt shook loose. When the fragment was clean and dry, the lab techs painted a tiny strip of Wite-Out on a side, then wrote the catalog number in the tiniest script with a special Rapidograph pen. My mom had elegant handwriting, the techs told me, so she often performed this task when she was working in the lab. I felt a flush of pride knowing the important work my mom and Bill were doing. They didn't have much, but I could see that archaeology was about something more important than money.

I sat on a stool, breathing in the trailers' smell of dirt and watery coffee on a hot plate, and watching Lorraine vibrate, mesmerized by her mechanical shaking and the water's tight, wiggly patterns across her surface. At the next turn, the tech nodded to me. I put my hand on the metal switch and pushed, and the machine pulsed into life. I steadied before it, craning my face in as I watched the whir of dirt breaking free in the water.

I would be coming back in the summer, and I anticipated that this was what my life would be like when I returned, going to the dig site with Bill or hanging out in the lab trailers with the techs and Lorraine and Francine. But that wasn't how it worked out.

That summer, my mom and Bill moved from the camp onto the reservation proper, outside the town of Nespelem, to a dot on the map called Keller and into a house they rented from Christine and Joe, who were elders of the Okanagan Nation. It was a very basic, well-worn little house, just plywood-and-cinder-block shelves, a couple of lamps, and Bill's turntable, but my mom had set it up nicely and it felt like home. No phone, but that wasn't unusual—phones were a luxury item we couldn't afford. The house was so far out we didn't even get real radio stations but listened to Bill's Cat Stevens and Steely Dan records. My room was a tiny sun porch off the kitchen, where I slept on a little metal folding army cot with a soft mattress.

There were no people around.

No archaeologists calling out to each other.

No young lab assistants ducking by outside the window.

No one.

My mom and Bill would pull out in the morning by 6:00 a.m. for the forty-five-minute drive to the camp, and I'd stay behind. There was no more talk of my doing any sifting at the dig site or hanging around the lab trailers at camp, and I took this in with some disappointment.

I did love the wild terrain outside the house, though, and at first it filled me up, helping me shake the cold, wet spring I had spent with my dad. A forest of grass, several feet taller than me, had a path through it leading down to the Sanpoil River. There were long-needled pine trees everywhere. After checking the fridge for RC Cola (every now and again I'd get lucky and there would be a forgotten one at the back), I'd head outside. I wore one piece of clothing that *entire* summer: a shiny cerulean-blue swimsuit with food spilled down the front like a little grease trail that ran from my mouth to my lap. I complemented it with either a beat pair of green tennis shoes or my mom's red striped flip-flops, which were too big. I had my own blue pair, but wearing my mom's made me feel close to her. The dogs would go bounding ahead, crashing through the grasses, looking to flush up any chasable, unsuspecting creature. They didn't get lucky much, so they just chased each other mostly, though we did see deer now and again. We had grasshoppers the size of staplers with underwings like striped blushing flamenco skirts. They came in gray, rust, mustard, and mauvish muted colors that blended with the ground so completely they always startled me when they flew up from under my feet. The path to the water was a mix of eolian sand (a tumbled, semi-opaque translucent substance deposited by the wind) and regular dirt that glinted when the sun hit it just right. The sides of the trail were lined with varied dry plants that grew up tall, almost creating a tunnel: pine grass, bluebunch wheatgrass, Idaho fescue, and some sages. The non-native plants blended right in: Russian tumbleweed sage, plantain, and flowering mullein, which dotted the edge of the trail like knights' dress swords held straight into the air, making my procession to the river seem very grand and elegant.

At the river, there was a fabulous swimming hole, big enough for three people. But there was almost always only me. There was no beach, but potato-sized, rounded-smooth river stones along the edge. I would go to my regular boulder, set down my towel, and immediately begin looking for bugs and animals. The creatures that most interested me were the caddis fly larvae we incorrectly called "periwinkles," small, rake-clawed little guys who live in tube casings made of silk that stays sticky underwater and attracts small stones, sand, snail shells, and plant debris. They looked to me like they lived in a sleeping bag made of collected turquoise rings. I'd watch the bats and the birds dip into the river to drink like they were stitching the water to the sky in lacy, swooping, baroque arcs. It was never boring, but despite all the life around me, I chafed at the isolation.

Our nearest neighbor was over a mile away. My mom and Bill didn't return until six at night. My bedtime was nine thirty or ten, depending, so I was only spending about *three hours a day* with other human beings, and then only my parents. I was beyond lonely. I was in a constant state of agitation and impatience: "How long till they get home?" As time went on it became a form of emotional starvation, like my stomach was eating its own lining in my longing for some species recognition and connection. I was lonely at my dad's house, too, but this was different, like being captive in an hourglass.

Sometimes my unhappiness came out in ways that still make me sad and ashamed. One time I got frustrated with my dog Sasha and "spanked" her for pretty much nothing. I immediately felt awful. I don't know where the anger flushed up from. Some shipwrecked frustration shrieking to be rescued way down in the darkest parts of my gizzard, maybe. Or maybe, too, I had inherited more of my mom's sparks of anger than I knew. I cried so hard, holding Sasha and rocking her back and forth on the plywood floor. I had broken my own heart by hitting my gentle, sweet friend. I went into the kitchen still sobbing and made her a glass of chocolate milk. She drank it from the cup in my hands as I blubbered, "I'm so sorry, I'm sorry, I'm so sorry, baby…"

We never spoke of my mom's "death" anymore, or her return. There was a dreamlike sweetness that hung around my visits to her and Bill. I had a kid's proprietary pleasure in her beauty, in the cozy arrangements she had made in the house, in eating cookies she'd baked. It was all my heart wanted, to be near her—and I moved carefully that summer, I see now, like if I made too much of a fuss I'd wake us from the dream. A couple of times I had mentioned to my parents that I missed them when they were away, but I had made light of it. I also knew they had to work—if they didn't work, we didn't eat, so why harp on it?

But that night, after lashing out at Sasha, I poured out what had happened and confessed that I was lonely and scared during the day. A few days later, I was in a car being driven to some friends of theirs who had kids. We arrived at the house, a nice trailer with lots of wood paneling and soft pine needles for a front yard, around eight in the morning. Once I got out of the car my parents drove off without a look back.

There were no adults around, just four kids. The oldest, maybe about ten years old, introduced himself to me as Danny, but his three sisters didn't even look up from the cartoons they were watching. They all just stared at the TV, three matching Tupperware bowls of cereal in their laps. Danny was a talker, and he gave me a tour of the house. He was a thin Indigenous kid with medium-length hair that fell around his ears, wearing jeans, a T-shirt, and off-brand tennis shoes, just like me. He must have been as lonely as me, too, because even though I was only seven *and* a girl he was still talking to me!

We went outside through the sliding glass door off the kitchen, to the sandy backyard full of wild plants skirting the pine forest. I saw animal tracks right by the back steps. "Wow! Are those deer? Do they come *that* close to your house?"

Danny looked at me with his face screwed up in disgust. "What? Am I supposed to be some kind of tracker?!" he spat indignantly.

What had I said wrong? Did he not like deer? It was only years later that I realized what that innocent question could have sounded like to an Indigenous kid, coming from this little white girl he'd just met. The moment passed and we went back inside. There would be no more talking about animals.

I soon found out why Danny was willing to talk to me.

"Do you like KISS?" he asked. You could hear the capital letters and the lightning bolt *S*'s just in how he said it.

"KISS? What's that?" (I didn't realize the song "Beth" I'd heard ten million times at the Bellingham roller rink was a KISS song.)

Danny ignited like a punk-lit sparkler as he launched into a lengthy, unselfconscious presentation of why KISS was the greatest band on the face of the fucking earth. He brought every KISS record he owned from his bedroom, laying them on the living room floor. The covers looked like horror comics.

The most terrifying one was the cover art for *Love Gun*. On it, the members of KISS were grouped in a single mass of unbridled, matter-of-fact demonic glee, crotches bulging, floating slightly above a pile of women melting into a salty, foggy sea of rock and roll ecstasy. At seven years old, I thought women painted as sex clowns in the throes of an "erotic swoon" looked almost exactly like people dying a painful death. (Just like the pictures of Christ at my gramma's Catholic church.) I thought the music must be about people being tortured by monsters and dying and was instantly *terrified* of KISS. Meanwhile, Danny's enthusiasm knew no empathy; I was his captive to be converted to KISS ARMY material, and he only had an afternoon to make a soldier out of me. I now understood why his little sisters did *not* engage in *any* way. They had learned not to make eye contact should they risk looking even a little ripe for KISS conversion. He made the trailer around us feel like the big top with KISS the star in all three rings, eating fire, blowing themselves out of cannons, riding T. Rexes, swallowing swords, and giving little boys rabies. He put on *Destroyer*, but the music made little impression on me—compared to the images on the album cover, it was underwhelming. Later in life I learned what made KISS great *and* hilarious, but it missed me then. Sadly, that day in the trailer had just been a little too much for me, so I didn't ask to go back. Fear is funny; it sometimes seems more possible to continue doing time in the lonely jail you know rather than rising above it to connect with others. This was one of those great defeats.

So I went back to being alone. All the time. I was desperate to find something new, to find a way to move through the day without feeling lost in time. There were brittle grayed wood shacks all around the property, but I had been told not to go near them because the place was literally crawling with rattlesnakes. Snakes could be coiled anywhere. I wasn't afraid of snakes, and I even liked them, but the protocol Bill told me to follow should I be bitten ran through my head endlessly: *Tie off the wound, ice it, and run (walk? crawl!?) immediately to the next house just over a mile away and ask to use their phone.* (The best part was that my stepdad had no idea whether our neighbors even *had* a phone!)

I didn't end up getting bitten that summer, but fuck if I didn't come close. And in the place I least expected: on the naked ground in the middle of the yard where there was nothing to hide under. One afternoon I saw my dark tabby kitty, Mamou, there so I walked over to pet her. As I reached for her, I heard the weirdest sound. I *knew* that sound. There was a big fat rattlesnake right in front of me. How had I not seen it?! Mamou had been casting a frozen stare over the snake, sizing it up as prey, and now I was in between them. In the millisecond my gaze rested on her I noticed her natural arrogance as she bristled to go into battle. She stood stock-still and her eyes became lasers. The sound of the snake's rattle buzzed like a swarm of cicadas, a shaky-poison-drag-your-ass-a-mile-after-I-bite-you-if-you-dare alarm.

Oh no.

Just when I was reaching the apex of my terror, Mamou moved to the left and distracted the snake, which followed her with its head. I began to back away slowly, then quickly, then I turned and sprinted to where my stepdad kept a sharp garden blade. I had to kill the snake before it killed Mamou. I grabbed the garden tool and ran back, but by the time I reached the spot where the snake had been, it was just Mamou, sitting there casually, cleaning a front paw. What had happened between them? Relief flooded my body, but I was so shaken, soon I was crying on the porch until Sasha came to comfort me. There would be no one home for *hours*.

There were little forays into the world now and again. Going into Grand Coulee with my parents for a burger on the weekend. Hearing the copper sparkly cinnamon sound of Rickie Lee Jones's "Chuck E's in Love" on the car radio. Driving to Omak to see *Bambi* in the theater in my stepdad's blue Ford F-150 with a homemade plywood camper on the back. My mom and Bill had gotten that truck as a wedding present from a friend. It had a giant fortune teller's eye painted on the sides of the camper top. Joni Mitchell's *Court and Spark* was permanently in the tape deck. We didn't get sick of it. Bill liked to call her "Moany Jitzell," which always made me laugh. Getting my ears pierced at a powwow was a big deal for me, too. You were basically an adult if you had your ears pierced, so I was *that* much closer to something. I didn't linger on the question of "what." Everything about that day at the powwow was incredible; the molten fry bread and frosty Cokes tasted like winning an award just for being alive.

But those rare excursions couldn't touch the bottomless loneliness of those days, the feeling that I was tiny, dwarfed by even the long grass. The pain of it was like a new brand, pressed down over the freshly healed brand of my mom's disappearing. The scar tissue screamed under my clothes. But I was a kid and this was our lot, as I was reminded by my dad in a stern voice if I ever complained about anything. All these things I occupied myself with seemed to take up no time at all. This was a different, softly pine-scented loneliness than when I was with my dad, one that was less harsh, witnessed by the countless eyes and ears of the nature around me, so I wasn't alone. But I was still stranded, still unwanted. The ways to be unwanted were inexhaustible, it seemed, and as a child I still had no clue how to claim a spot for myself in the world.

Chapter 5

Neko Case Rm. 16

The local news glowed on the TV. A young woman's face flashed on the screen. It was a high school photo, and in it she smiled with happy eyes and chunky white teeth—and the smile stayed there, frozen on the screen, as the newscaster described the shallow grave where her body had been found. She was eighteen and had been missing for three months. She was the eighth victim of the man who would become known as the Green River Killer. I absorbed the distant way the newscaster spoke of the girl, the disapproval contained in the words "last seen walking from a motel." The victims were never referred to as women or even people, just "prostitutes." Never even as "children," though many of them were. In all, the Green River Killer would murder at least seventy women around Seattle and Tacoma, and he'd go uncaptured for almost twenty years. Meanwhile, his victims' short lives were boiled down to what pieces of clothing were found in the woods: a single sock, a pair of flowered underwear. As I watched the news with my dad, the dead girls' essences would vaporize through the living room like rubbing alcohol off a dirty cotton ball. It screwed up my breathing. They were like dry sticks being fed into a savage furnace forever.

We'd moved to Vancouver, Washington, for my dad's new job a few years earlier, in time for me to start fourth grade. The house we lived in was a yellow-brown smear, most of the rooms in too bad a condition to use. My dad said he was going to fix them, but he never got around to it. The walls were pockmarked here, water damaged there; the bad mildewy carpet puckered into sneering ridges. There wasn't a single nice, finished place to sleep or even sit. The only exception was the grow room in the basement. My dad's pot-growing space was tidy and clean.

"Never under any circumstances tell anyone this exists, period!" he told me like I was already in trouble.

Were the police coming?

I knew I would most likely be home alone if that happened and was terrified I was going to get my dad thrown in jail if I wasn't a good enough liar. That fear hummed in my body constantly, somehow joining forces with the baseline dread I felt from watching the violent images flash across the news. And there was a third dread, eager to mingle with the other two.

I'd just seen a B-thriller on TV called *Where Have All the People Gone?* In it, the earth was ruined by solar flares, and the vaporized people were all reduced to piles of salt trailing out of whatever clothing they'd been wearing when they'd been radiated. And all the animals on earth went crazy. I looked around the dank carpet I was sitting on. Our dogs would sometimes pee on it, and me or my dad would pour salt on the puddle to "absorb it." The idea was that later you'd vacuum it up and there would be no smell. It didn't work, and we seldom vacuumed it up anyway. All around me were piles like little sand trap anthills that we just stepped over or on; the trails of salt reminded me of vaporized people.

I knew when my dad got home from work he'd go straight to the bong in front of his chair and take several deep hits. Drugs were his way of coming home, then disappearing again, to some place better. It was obvious to me even then he was escaping me, and his life. He wasn't even thirty yet and seemed so old. If he wasn't in his chair, he was in his room, which I was too afraid to enter. It had a curtainless window that looked into the dark and creepy garage. It was like the window to a bad dream, just a frame for clown-faced killers.

I snapped off the TV, maneuvering around desiccated bodies, and up the flight of dingy, forest-green-carpeted stairs to my attic room. It had a pitched roof and severely slanted ceilings. My Scholastic puppy and kitten posters sagged like flying squirrels from their silver thumbtacks. The most important feature of my room was the Emerson clock radio I had gotten for Christmas. It was tuned to Portland's KMJK 107.7, the Magic FM. It was the rock station that played everything from 10cc to the Clash. Quarterflash, Bill Withers, the Spinners, the Motels, Romeo Void, Blondie, and the Pretenders, and a bizarre mix of Top 40. More women were played on KMJK than the other stations, but I wasn't doing that chronic math in my mind yet—at least not consciously. I kept the radio on all the time. I woke up to it, and I fell asleep to it. I sang to it, too. I listened to the radio and drew pictures of horses, waiting for my dad to come home, even though he hardly breathed my air.

As long as I can remember I have loved music. A huge cliché for a musician's story, I know, but I had no idea how crazy I was about it even as it was burning me down. I listened to it as much as possible; it filled every nook and cranny of my life and nothing fun was worth doing if there wasn't music being played in the background. It was important in a way I couldn't see, let alone acknowledge. All through grade school I loved music class. We sang some really weird religious songs and lots of show tunes I didn't understand the lyrics to, but I didn't care. I even liked the rhythm exercises and "Ta Ta Tee Tee Ta." The joy of singing to a chronically shy kid is a priceless outlet. In class it was easy to be anonymous because everyone *had* to sing. I could sing my little pigeon-chested heart out! I could hide in plain sight and I loved it.

I brought records to school: a Go-Go's "We Got the Beat" 45 and *The Best of Blondie*. I had bought both with my own money at the Fred Meyer on Fourth Plain Boulevard in Vancouver. Lunch recess was for music zone-out, and I'd head to the library with my records under my arm, carefully labeled *Neko Case Rm. 16*. It was always needly rain outside, and I never had a proper coat, so I didn't even entertain the thought of going out to play. And besides, I didn't yet have any steady friends at this new school, so there was no one to play *with*. The Pacific Northwest has a cold like no other place. It seeps through your clothes and keeps you cold like your own personal ghost has moved in. There are mildew and wet windowsills all winter. Hardly anyone I knew could afford proper heat.

The library was all the way down the hall past all the younger grades. It had big windows and epic droopy cedars outside looking like Mr. Snuffleupagus. There were green and brown corduroy bean bags to sit on and read books. I went in as much as I could. I'd post up at the tanklike record player, which stood side by side in a military line with several indestructible army-issue-looking cassette tape machines, the kind with the handles on the front, solid and ready for field duty. Grab that handle and lob it like a grenade straight over the Iron Curtain! We will end the Cold War with rock and roll! That's what Russia wants, right? Well, shit! We got *plenty* to go round! I would secure my giant headphones, like a helicopter pilot's, and place my record onto the turntable and drop the needle on the song I wanted to listen to.

Have you ever seen a cat staring at a particular spot on the wall, absorbed by something you can't see? That was what I was like when the needle dropped on the record. My whole body would enter a state of suspended animation, a rapt sort of tension. Let's say the song was "Atomic" by Blondie, which I was obsessed with that year. My body remained there in the library but the heart of me was enmeshed in its sound of punk Morricone disco. It sounded to me like Debbie Harry was singing off the edge of a cliff to a sunset she was wooing. Then there was "Ooohhhhhh, your hair is beautiful...tonight..." What a vague and bizarre statement! So many stories could be happening under that line, and I was a prisoner to all their possible meanings. Kids might come and go near me. An adult might walk by. I wouldn't ever notice, I was so fixed on the music.

I dropped the needle on that song over and over, until the bell rang and snapped me back into my school self.

After school let out, I'd make the cold walk home, sometimes stopping at the 7-Eleven for a cola Slurpee, which did nothing to warm me, but sometimes the buzz of the sugar made me forget. The street we lived on was crappy and rife with potholes. Walking it was a video game I would always lose. There was always some poor possum that had its brains squashed out in the gutter and litter everywhere. I remember once having shoes with blown-out soles that I had to wear because no others fit. My feet would be soaked coming and going; the blue of the leather off-brand tennis-shoe emblem discolored my socks.

When I'd get home my dad would still be at work. Which meant I had to remember my key. One time I got home and had to poop so badly, but then realized I had no key. I ran around back hoping maybe my dad had forgotten to lock the back door to the garage. Nope. I shit myself right then. I immediately started to cry out of shame. I was so mad about the crying *and* the soiling of my pants that I became an angry little commando. I knew what to do: My dad watched a *lot* of crime shows. I took off my right shoe and then my wet sock. I wound the sock around my fist like people did when they were breaking and entering and smashed a pane out of the window of the back door. I reached through and let myself in, dealt with shitting my pants and then began to cry in earnest again because I knew my dad was going to kill me for breaking the window.

If I got *in* the house without incident, I would throw my books down, greet the dogs, and get something to eat. I always entered the kitchen with hope, but rarely did we have anything in the cabinets or fridge. And if there was a bag of Cheetos or something equally awesome, then I couldn't stop eating it until it was gone. But the Cheetos days were rare. We usually only had dehydrated potato flakes or cake mix, which I would eat dry, out of the box. I still remember the feeling of ripping the package open with my teeth. The immediate sensation was paper, then that super-thin plastic that would get stuck near my gums, a feeling that still haunts me, my skin crawling as I imagine it. This was never satisfying, just desperate. I was just so hungry and *bored*. I'd eat a bit, feel a bit sick, then move on. If I was really desperate, pancake mix or even flour would suffice. A few times I ate raw rice and pasta.

The magic self-soothe opium was eating *while* watching TV. We had two TVs, but only one worked, a tiny eight-inch black-and-white one perched right on top of a broken gargantuan color one. I watched *Gilligan's Island* (which I *hated*), *The Brady Bunch*, *Bewitched*, Warner Bros. cartoons, and *Tom and Jerry*, too. *The Flintstones* and *I Love Lucy*, and *The Addams Family* and *The Munsters*. But if I didn't change the channel fast enough, the local news would flash on, with the grim images of police and yearbook photos of victims, and I would try not to think of the window in my dad's bedroom that looked out into that darkness.

Hour after hour, I sat there for *years* in the freezing-cold living room of our freezing-cold house, on the stained, rust-colored carpet in the middle of piles of pet hair and salt, eyes glazed, staring at the tiny black-and-white TV.

Here's something I'd do: I'd pick fleas off the dogs and cat, bite their tiny heads off, and spit them into the grill of the shitty Superelectric Instaheat space heater, where they would mingle with dog hair and fry next to the fluorescent orange ribbon of heat, making a smell that was too disgusting to even try to describe.

I only used my teeth, so I didn't taste fleas, but I may as well have. I was reduced to a beast, a low-grade beast stewing in its own juice, waiting for something I couldn't name. Around the edges of my life, the Green River Killer stalked the forest, and his victims continued to flash across the TV screen at night.

There was one bright spot during that time, a Thanksgiving I got to visit Mom and Bill on the Colville reservation, a burst of radiance in the middle of a gray field. When I arrived, the snow was falling, and Sasha had had a litter of eight puppies in various color and spot combinations. They had the softest little bed under a table by the front window, already surrounded by Christmas lights. They smelled hot and sweet like bread dough.

I was so glad to be back at Mom and Bill's, the three of us together as a family. The air smelled like pine needles and turkey soup, not burned fleas and dog hair and piss. Everything was in its place: pottery on the shelves, found bird feathers, special rocks and animal bones laid out like precious artifacts in a museum. There was a fire going in the woodstove casting a glorious light on the wall behind, like a dancing amber figure on the wall of a cave. There were teacups on the table and homemade cookies.

The couch was covered by familiar blankets and my mom's craft bag was out. I loved to pull out all the skeins of embroidery floss and sort them in rainbow order, then separate out the ones I wanted to use. I'd find a piece of creamy muslin and smash it onto the embroidery hoop, then pull its little skirts out to the sides to make it taut. Then I would make a light pencil sketch of what I wanted to embroider on the muslin: *A cat's face? A flower?* My mom had taught me how to do this on previous visits, and I was experienced enough now to start on my own.

One night I was drawing pictures with jewel-colored embroidery floss as Bill and my mom read and the stereo played. Suddenly I had a question.

"Mom, what is the difference between an alligator and a crocodile?"

She wasn't sure, but then I saw her smile. She'd remembered that when you have a question about nature, you can ask the Smithsonian in Washington, DC.

"Really?"

"Yes!" she said. "All you have to do is write them a letter."

Looking up, Bill yelled from across the room, "Ask 'em if they both crap in the water!"

Mom rolled her eyes at him, and I laughed.

Mom got a piece of paper and a pencil. She assumed the role of my secretary and took down my inquiry word for word, then we signed our names officially on the bottom and sealed it in an envelope.

"I'll mail it tomorrow," she said as I licked a stamp with a meadowlark on it and stuck it on the envelope.

We never heard back from the Smithsonian, but that night was a little window into how I wanted our lives to be every night: fed, warm, creative, loving, and laughing. It was in such stark contrast to my life with Dad. I would try to hold the images and feelings inside my body when I was back home, sitting on the filthy rust carpet, but they never could keep the cold and the fear and the loneliness at bay. In thrall to the cozy, happy house, I would almost forget that she had ever died—so total was my joy that she'd come back. If I felt anything provisional about her allowing me to draw close to her, I would tamp it down, put it outside the house like a bag of garbage.

Chapter 6

Demolition Derby

It's summer, and I'm hanging upside down over the midway of the Northwest Washington Fair, crammed in the cage of a ride called the Zipper. My cousins Brent and Jay are in the next cages over, and we scream to each other.

Brent: "I can't believe thissssss."

Jay: "Holy shiiiiiiiiiiiiiiiiiiit."

Me: "This is awesommmmmmmme."

It's not what we're saying that matters, not really—our voices are just lassos connecting us, carrying our love for the Zipper back and forth to each other. It's our singing. This isn't the first time we've been up here today. Not the fourth. It's the seventh time—and we're still shouting as loud as the first ride of the day. I love that my cousins are near me, but I love, too, having the cage to myself. At the top of the ride, as the Zipper pauses to change its violent direction, swaying just a little, my dirt-blond hair flies straight up into a witch's broom. The breeze moves past my cheeks and dries the tears being pulled from centrifugal force out the sides of my eyes. My fish-eye view of the midway and grandstand below swims before me.

I have the same reverence for the mechanical ingenuity of the Zipper as I had for the sonic vibration machines, Lorraine and Francine, back at the Columbia River dig-site camp. It looks something like a windmill with a teeter-totter of cages strapped to its top. The teeter-totter part is a series of closed elongated ovals that spin; then, as if that wasn't enough terror, you spin along the track of the oval in a single cage. That's THREE objects spinning within and along each other at once. It throws the g-force and the centrifugal force all off kilter, which is *horrifyingly* fun!

My cousins and I were expert spinners. The whole time we've been shouting, we've been spinning in our cages:

"I got five times!"

"Six times!"

Together, we dream of being professional Zipper riders, touring with the fair as it makes its way from stop to stop around the country. Decked out in astronaut-like suits, we would appear before the ride at different times across the day, on hand to demonstrate its myriad wonders as well as show off our masterful ability to make the cages spin. It's only too bad that such a career doesn't exist.

As I hang upside down, the warbled, disembodied notes of a country song float up from the bandshell stage. As my grandma loved to remind me, Loretta Lynn had lived not so long before in the nearby town of Custer, and I'd once heard her perform while I was hanging upside down on the Zipper.

The distortion of the distance and movement made Loretta sound half superstar, half bawling calf as she belted out "You Ain't Woman Enough (to Take My Man)," which was made even more surreal by the psychedelic pedal steel syrup warping behind her.

This year had something just as special in store for us.

My dad (like my mom) was a middle child, with an older sister and a younger one. His older sister was Nancy, and it was her sons, Brent and Jay, who were my regular comrades at the fair. They lived about twenty minutes away from me back in Vancouver in a little suburb called Hazel Dell. My cousins were rowdy and fought each other like crazy. They also loved each other like crazy, but any stunt worth doing was worth taking too far. Someone usually got hurt. No weapon was off limits—elbows, knees, pee, furniture—you name it. One time Brent threw some wet dog shit at Jay and was laughing his head off about it. Jay scooped different dog shit off the ground so fast and in one round movement hit Brent right in the side of his laughing mouth. Yes, some went in. There were tears. I did not engage in any of the physical danger, but I did help facilitate it. Everything seemed worth it for the hysterical laughter afterward.

My cousins' parents were divorced, too, but we never talked about it. We watched cartoons together. We browsed through the Sears and Zellers catalogs for *hours* and marked what we wanted for Christmas. We rode bikes, built jumps and forts, and played outside when the weather permitted. We used to love watching *CHiPs* and *The Dukes of Hazzard* and drinking root beer (pronounced "Rut-Beer" in our trashy western Washington accents). All three of us liked to play cars and trucks. Our dogs even liked each other. They had a dark gray standard poodle named Sam, a lovely smarty-pants who lived to be a thousand.

The boys had a cool tree fort in the backyard that their dad had built, and it was from this fort that we watched Mount St. Helens blow up. We were supposed to go to Horseshoe Lake that day, but the sonic boom that announced the catastrophic volcanic eruption ended that plan quickly. We watched the column of blue-gray ash rise higher and higher, straight up into the sky, taller than we'd ever seen *anything* go, until eventually it began to taper eastward. We wondered if the lava was gonna come for us and were thankful to the point of being smug that we were holed up in a tree house. The eruption of Mount St. Helens was all that was on the news, except for the latest update about the Green River Killer. Afterward, the three of us gathered talc-like ash off the ground and put it in jars and labeled it "Mount St. Helens, May 18th, 1980" and took it to science period at school, just like every single other kid in the area.

The Northwest Washington Fair, three hours north in Lynden, where Gramma Case lived, was the highlight of our year. It went on for days, and we lived and breathed for it. Gramma Case worked at the Eastern Star hamburger booth, and we slept at her house during the fair's run, showing up at her booth first thing in the mornings. Those older ladies worked their asses off in teams of four and five to keep up with the demand. The burgers were delicious and the smell of the fried onions lorded it over the midway. My cousins and I would inhale our free burgers and Cokes, then hit the ground running.

There is little in life so sweet as having some money in your pocket and strolling the grounds of a fair. We were inexhaustible, high on smells and tastes and sights and sounds. We were wide-open sensory recorders ablaze with wonder. Sure, we had seen it all before, but somehow it always managed to seem sparkling and new.

First-day tradition was to go through *every* exhibition hall, even the dairy machinery expo, which was outside. There would always be a cow up on a pedestal munching hay while being milked by a four-pronged suction robot with see-through cylinders so you could watch the milk coming *out* of the cow. It looked like four tiny washing machine windows, revealing the alternately pink- and milk-colored scene inside as it agitated the cow's teats. The cow was always unperturbed and patient, content with her snack. The milking expo was always *so* clean, nothing like the *actual* barns the milk came from. Half my family were dairy farmers, and their barns had shit *everywhere*. The new, surgically precise world of milk extraction fooled a lot of visitors and likely sold a lot of pricey machinery to farmers on credit.

There was no set rule as to how we tackled the fair layout, but we seemed to move in certain routes. Midsize farm animals were first priority—goats, pigs, etc.—then on to cows, their dark liquid eyes so soft, their big vinyl noses so glossy-wet. There was always a team of eager 4-H teens and preteens to feed the animals and shovel away the poop. They all wore jackets with 4-H logos on them, and I wanted to join so badly and have one of those jackets with my name on it, too, but all I had at home was a dog and a cat, no goats or pigs or cows. The ache inside me was painful. I would eye the 4-H kids, shy and hungry for what they had. I yearned to look after these critters in all their many shapes and sizes and gain access to their particular temperaments and personalities. I wanted to be able to say the word "urine" without cracking up, like a livestock expert. I wanted to lead a young steer out of a show ring by a fat cotton lead rope attached to a pristine blue halter, the creature following me, trusting and obedient because I had worked hard day after day to bond with him.

Next came the high point of the daylight hours: the equine barns. First were regular riding horses and ponies of every conceivable shape and color. It was a cruel paradise of longing, the pinching, sweet smell of horses driving me to controlled, low-level insanity. I would float along somehow, despite being crushed under the weight of my love for them, like I was walking on a different planet with its own rules of gravity. The anxiety of needing to make sure I saw them *all* was real, too, electricity running along the outside of a wire, dangerous and immediate. The biggest thrill for me was the team barns; there was every size of horse, small Shetland ponies to the great draft giants. There were chuck wagon races, six to eight horses each, the teams comprised of identically colored equines with special fancy show harnesses in bright reds and blues and blacks, studded with silver cabochons. They looked so smart and professional! The pony teams came in every color: dappled gray, bay, roan, dun, paint, Appaloosa, black, and on and on. I loved seeing them in their temporary show stalls, fancy carved wooden nameplates on the doors. They all had names like "Merlin" and "Comet."

The best I saved for last. Entering the draft horse hall took my breath away. There they were, looking like quiet, prehistoric giant geniuses. Their stomachs were at eye level, and I loved the topography of their bellies, studying how their hair grew and stretched into tidal patterns; it curled and cowlicked and highlighted the shapes of their muscles. Their haunches were like sides of beef, their tails either a waterfall of clean, conditioned wiry glory or tied up into a braided stump of a bun like the hair of a German Hofbräu waitress. Their feet were larger than dinner plates, but they moved so gracefully, and copious manes thatched their powerful, mountainous necks. Their huge, calm eyes would briefly regard me and I would imagine a real connection. I wanted to live at the fair with them forever, to brush and feed them for the rest of my life. Leaving the last barn full of Percherons would break my heart every time. I imagined curling up like a cat on their warm dappled gray and shiny blue-black butts and dreaming.

"I'll come back," I'd say, lingering at the barn exit. Leaving always required a Coke or a lemonade to bolster my soul. Maybe fry bread or even a funnel cake, too. Then I'd travel with my cousins to the hobby barns, a soothing comedown from my bittersweet high. We'd rush past the construction paper and poster board 4-H displays to get to the flowers and the crafts. The huge dahlias were the best. They were so grand without seeming vain somehow. I loved the dark ones with their hints of red and magenta peeking out from their sea urchin faces.

There was every craft imaginable! Every kind of sewing and woodcarving. There were preserves and desserts, paintings and drawings, and even portraits made of different-colored beans. *Anyone* could enter, even me! I loved the ribbons awarded in all their bright, important colors, the royal blueberry purple the highest honor. Some of the crafts had even been awarded silver cups with feathery engraving on them. This was as good as it got, and it was truly grand! One year I entered two drawings of, surprise, horses. I ended up winning a ribbon, but I don't remember what color, which surprises me because the fair was the highlight of my world. I felt so important having *real* art in the craft hall. I was ten and now legitimately a part of the fair. Maybe I never won a ribbon and I just *needed* to so badly that I've conjured one? It's funny how our desires can cut a memory groove like on a record.

Once we had seen all the quilts on the walls and chain saw lawn art, we went to visit the poultry and rabbit sheds. There were even doves and pigeons, so sleek and soft looking I was desperate to hold one in my hands, but I never did. I imagined the warm birds nestled into your palms must feel like the taste of chocolate milk.

At some point during the day, I'd slip away from my cousins and head over to the carousel horses. I was too old for the ride, so my gangly legs flopped out sideways all the way to the metal plates on the floor. "I *will* have a horse someday," I would pray, my forehead cooling against the metal pole.

As the sun started to go down, the carnival lights snapped on, brilliant red and yellow and green neon streaks that somehow made all the sounds and smells even more intoxicating. We sauntered down the midway, eyeing the scam carny games, the bowls of beta fish lined up on a splintery plywood table like tragic, bulging raindrops. The rides that frantically whorled around us were as painted and pin-striped as hot rods in brilliant rainbow aqua neons, metal flakes suspended in their glossy depths like diamonds. Whenever I hear "Crocodile Rock" by Elton John or "Poor Poor Pitiful Me" by Linda Ronstadt I'm transported immediately back to the night midway of the fair.

It was a place of safe heartbreak, greasy food, hypnotizing smells, never-ending boulevards of lights and possibilities. The old rural world by day, followed by the modern temptations of controlled danger at night. There were feathered roach clips, balloon animals, invisible dog leashes, rainbow-sand-filled bottles dressed as exotic birds, giant stuffed animals so overfilled with Styrofoam beads they squeaked when you touched them. It was all magic but rooted in the homey realness of things like canned pickles in Ball jars and fresh steaming flat patties of cow shit.

The fair held most of the wonders of the world, and we had seen pretty much all of them. What else could there be after all *this*? I'll tell you what: demolition derby.

Every day brought elimination heats for the demolition derby, with the winners advancing toward the final nighttime championship that closed out the fair. My cousins and I often attended these first heats, but we never much cared who ultimately won: We just loved to watch them smash up the cars. This year, though, we found ourselves transfixed by the heroic maneuvers of a blue and orange sedan, its Day-Glo pink number painted boldly on both sides: 26.

Now, at a demolition derby, everyone *knows* the station wagons have the advantage, especially behemoths like the Ford Country Squires and the Mercury Colony Parks. Even an Aspen could win the day! Their back ends girded by extra metal, prowling and waiting, pretending to stall between disabled vehicles, revving their massive V-8 engines like they were helpless. Then they'd suddenly launch themselves back into the fray. BAM! Out of nowhere would come the bludgeoning hammer of a Buick Estate, the largest station wagon ever built.

Game over.

I saw so many cars taken out this way it was old hat, and I never held out hope for the sedans.

So it was a pleasant surprise when 26 won the first match. The next day it did it again. This had to be a fluke? By the third victory, my cousins and I were devoted fans, committed to watching every match from then on. It's all we talked about, and thanks to our gramma and free admission, we went loyally every day, the most glorious demolition derby bender *any* ten-year-old *anywhere* could hope for. Six days in a row! Number 26 kept winning and we kept screaming our guts out, so high on carbon monoxide and adrenaline we were loopy. Whenever the enormous yellow tractor with the two forks on the front end came to remove the *huge* log, creating an opening in the circle "pit" of the derby ring and signaling the start of the match, I would feel my metallic blood pressure rise. I wanted annihilation.

And then it was the final night. We sat in the artificial daytime of the grandstand, moths and bats embroidering evasive flight paths in the floodlights; the smell of gas and exhaust, petroleum grease machine lubricant, burning tire rubber and summer and popcorn in the air; the burn of a Coca-Cola in my nose; the soft breeze blowing across our faces. The wooden benches were packed ass-to-ass, the smell of human sweat and cigarettes hanging thick. I was so tense I chewed all the ice out of my empty soda.

The male announcer's distorted voice was pitched high as he called the cars into the ring for one last showdown. Everyone cheered as they paraded in. When 26 entered the ring, my cousins and I stood and shrieked until our voices strained and cracked. I don't remember the exact sequence of events that led to the eventual elimination of every car but two, but I do remember breathless silences from the crowd as cars smashed into each other with deafening crunches. I remember tiny fires spurting out of engines and the air horn signaling for the time-out flag to twirl as the pit crews in fire suits ran over to extinguish the flames in a daredevil dramatic stream of cream-colored flame retardant.

Debris littered the dirt corral: mufflers, tires, and even whole cars with their drivers still stuck inside. They would have to wait to be cut out later. It was now an obstacle course as well as a derby pit. Some cars were stuck together like mating bugs, unable to break free. The drivers had no choice but to put out their orange flags on the roof and wait.

In the end, Number 26 pulled a truly believable fake breakdown. We thought it was over; a done deal. But at the last second it roared to life, sparks coming out of the tailpipe, dealing the death blow to the hearse-looking station wagon that was looking to end it. Number 26 pushed that beast right up and over one of the giant logs enclosing the arena. My cousins and I just couldn't believe it! We were still on our feet screaming as the wrecker went in and pulled the defeated wagon off the log and dragged it away.

We floated out of the fair and slept like the dead that night. We were so *deeply* satisfied, our little hearts full of triumph.

Years later, in the early 2000s, I was on tour in my beloved GMC Rally van with my band of friends on the way to a show. Somewhere in the middle of Indianapolis, on a scorching summer day, I looked to my right and saw a man in his driveway welding some crash bars onto his flat-black-primered demo derby car. On the roof was a trophy he must have won the year before. There it was, just gleaming its ass off in the oppressive Midwestern summer heat like it was the sun itself. It was so beautiful and heart-wrenching; I wanted to *be* that man so *badly* I would have turned around to help him weld had we not been late for sound check.

Chapter 7

Reel to Reel

I was lying with the dogs on the floor near the space heater. My dad and I were still living in the yellow-brown house with all its unfinished rooms. It was always cold, and this was the one warm spot. The dogs were drowsing, and I was only half listening as my uncle Junior's voice sawed away. "You told me you did it, and then I came in and you hadn't done it," he said to my aunt. When she answered, he said, "Don't whine, Mama Bear, you lied about it…" My uncle liked to tell people not to whine *and* accuse them of lying.

Junior was a tall man, taller even than my dad, and broad shouldered. Whenever I looked up at him from my spot on the floor, he looked like a pillar of sculpted lard. Black hair, black eyes, and a belligerent way of swaggering into rooms and bestriding them. He had a tattoo of an eagle on his right bicep and kept a knife-sharpening whetstone hanging on his belt. He was married to my dad's younger sister, and I'd see him over at my Gramma Case's sometimes. Even as a child I could tell that he wasn't right in a way that was frightening. Now older, I was able to be more specific in what it was about him that seemed peculiar. Like if he was absent for a while he'd claim it was because he was off doing "dangerous government work," yet he was also somehow always broke. Or that he, an adult, would be competitive with my cousins and me, and took an obvious gloating pleasure in cutting us down for any perceived infraction.

And now he was living with us. He, my aunt Carol, and my little cousin Darla had taken up residence in the rooms across the hall from my upstairs bedroom. I would lie in bed and hear him booming and bristling around. The whole house seemed to quake with him. One thing seemed certain: When Junior was there it wasn't really our house anymore.

My little cousin Darla was a sweet, curious little kid, and she'd follow me around, wanting to hang out. I was her older cousin, after all, still a kid but one with makeup (not that I was allowed to wear it) and a bedroom to myself. I loved her, but there was no way I was gonna admit it to the adults.

"She's bugging me again!" I'd yell from my bedroom when she came in.

Silence.

Then my aunt's weed-addled premature old-lady voice would crab, "Neko, don't be so stingy. Try to share with her."

"I was talking to my *dad!*" I'd yell back.

I would look over at Darla, a confident little being with brown hair and a sweet moon face. *How can you not fucking hate this?!* I wondered. She didn't know yet how shitty our lives were.

I didn't want to wreck it for her. I looked into her hazel eyes, and I just couldn't tell her that these people were broken.

My dad had always been a strange, lonely, timid man. He loved dark justice movies like *Billy Jack*, listening to records with giant headphones on, and making tiny Cheez-It and peanut butter sandwiches on flimsy paper plates and eating them while smoking weed in front of the TV. Whatever his faults, at his core he was a peaceful person who was into camping, working on cars, and drawing. He liked to laugh. Richard Pryor and Robin Williams were his favorite comedians. But after my uncle's arrival on the scene, something shifted in him, like he was afraid to defy Junior.

My dad was clearly feeling lost. Even the comforts of his basement grow room weren't enough to make up for what a long, dry, sad time it had been without my mom or her love. Junior and Carol were Seventh-Day Adventists, and my dad decided he needed to get deeper with religion. In other words, it was Junior's idea. I can see how it all happened. A psychological bully, Junior seemed drawn, like so many other white men before him and since, to religion as a great way to manipulate and control the people around him. There were rules, and he was in charge of making sure we followed them, even if he didn't fully adhere to them himself. I have no idea where in his nefarious travels he had found Seventh-Day Adventism, but our lives were about to get *dark* and very limited. Gone were the days of sitting in the living room together, laughing at a movie like *Stir Crazy* or listening to Heart's *Little Queen*. In the months after Junior's arrival, things that had been wholesome before, and occasionally connected me to my dad, suddenly became "obscene."

When the rules of this new religion weren't trifling and petty, they were fiery and terrifying. It introduced the idea of Satan into our sad, shabby house with its incomplete, caved-in rooms, a version of the devil that was new to me, not just a generic force, but a REAL demon who was everywhere. He was like the Green River Killer that way—a malevolent presence skirting the edges of your everyday life, waiting to snatch you up and harm you.

And of course Junior didn't do dumb shit halfway, so he plunged into the specialty niche world of getting reel-to-reel tapes of "edgy" young pastors who would preach about the *real* devil at length, describing him in gruesome detail and all the different ways he would hurt us. Who knew, Satan might even be outside your house *right now*, walking down your shitty little street on this gray drizzly afternoon to pick you up and send you straight to hell to burn forever—as if your life didn't already suck hard enough. My little body was in a constant thrumming fight-or-flight vibration of "FUCK. THIS."

One night, as some pastor named Todd droned on about my eternal burning to come, I cracked. From my bedroom I yelled, "Turn it OFF! I'm afraid! I can't sleep!!"

I don't know where I summoned the courage from, but I think it had to do with a friend I had made in second grade, Penny Bowling, a tomboy like me.

Penny lived at the end of the street in a heavily used Victorian with her parents and an absolute army of siblings that poured in and out of the house all day. In fact, I'm not even sure I ever saw her parents. Just these brothers and sisters, of all ages, flowing about. They were a tight bunch, and I had the sense that with so many older siblings, Penny couldn't help but grow up a little faster—all the kids' interests blending together inside that giant, dilapidated house.

I liked Penny, even though her collection of horror comics scared me, and we spent our time happily playing like the semi-genderless kids we were. One sunny spring day, we were in her room when we heard some shouting. We poked our heads out of her doorway and confirmed that a big commotion was happening somewhere in front of the house, and we hustled our bony asses down the endless staircase to the front lawn.

Outside, a squad car was parked in the driveway on the "this is no joke, somebody's in trouble" diagonal.

Penny and I stood in the yard. By then, kids of all ages were streaming out of the house like hornets from a nest, and all of them, down to the youngest, were shouting at the cop: "YOU FUCKING PIG!!!"

They were like ravens harassing a hawk that had come too near their nest, surrounding the scene. I should have taken the opportunity to count them, but I was caught up in the emergency and so shocked by their bravery! *And* by their swearing! I was still so young, I was also absorbing the new idea that a cop appearing in your driveway could be a bad thing. I didn't yet know how evil cops could be; in my mind, policemen were still cute cartoons in schoolbooks who helped you find your cat or the gentle milquetoasts on the show *Adam-12*. I had never actually *met* one. But here was one, and the Bowling kids had him surrounded, shouting over and over again:

"YOU FUCKING PIG!!"

Finally, the officer flushed out and cuffed one of Penny's brothers, a lanky blond kid who protested loudly the whole way to the car. Later that day, I asked Penny why her brother was taken away.

"Aw," Penny explained, a bit tired, "they said he stole something, but he didn't do it."

She was used to this. And my first seed of rebellion was sown. You don't always have to take it lying down, it seemed? It was that vital observation, stored away for years, that I drew on to finally get my dad to turn off the terrifying, booming voice of the doom-loving pastor that echoed through our house.

To my dad's credit, he did turn it off, but the damage was already done. During this time, it felt like I was continuously yelling across a chasm to my dad, like he had become a permanent sleepwalker in our house, and I couldn't make sense of it. He and my aunt Carol had a strange dependence on each other that made me uncomfortable. He couldn't do anything without looking to her for approval. Years later I would come to understand this, but I didn't then. It was just another mystery, and it made him seem like more of a kid than I was—fragile and off, cowering in his own house, afraid of a bully like Junior.

Junior wasn't the only bully in my life at this time. There was also a block bully, Bob Abbott, who used to chase me on his bicycle: a yellow banana-seat bike with ape hangers that was too small for him. It seemed trapped under his cruel bulk.

He lived kitty-corner to us, in a chipped-up, skanky, and run-down house like mine, with piles of trash and car bones in the dirt-patch yard. Bob Abbott did not go to my school, which I assumed was because he was too mean. He seemed at *least* three grades older than me, so I couldn't figure out why he wanted to mess with me anyway. Wasn't I beneath his notice?

I'd be walking home from school as usual, feet wet, small, with a heavy backpack. He would see me from a couple of blocks away and a Joker smile would spread across his face. Shoving his handlebars in my direction, he'd make a beeline for me. I swear to god he made a wake ripple across the asphalt.

He would ride at me as fast as he could, tiny bike slapping from side to side like windshield wipers as he built up speed. He would get as close as possible, so I'd have to dive out of the way. He'd graze me with a handlebar or kick me with his foot, leaving bruises. The rushing tuna-cat-food wind of him always scared and humiliated me. I thought for sure he'd run me over and I'd get mangled in his chain, and lose a finger or worse.

One day I was headed home as usual, on yet another drizzly afternoon, when soon enough, Bob barreled toward me like a bull in a Bugs Bunny cartoon. Ahead, not far past him, I saw Aunt Carol's dog, Stonia, a good-sized Rhodesian Ridgeback, in our yard. Carol had told me Stonia was a good guard dog, and while my aunt lied about a *lot* of things, pretty much everything, really, she did *not* lie about dogs. I was desperate, so I played the only card I was holding.

"Stonia, sic 'em!" I screamed.

In slow motion, I saw her explode off the mark like a greyhound. It was beautiful. She reached him in a few not-fuckin'-around strides, grabbed his pant leg in her teeth, and pulled like a roping horse with fangs. She nearly took him off his bike with her first backward thrust. She knew not to bite his flesh, and when she realized she had him off balance she let go. He rattled his bike frame back upright and didn't stop pedaling until he was out of sight. Bob Abbott was *afraid*, and he never chased me again.

Bullies could be vanquished. I saw it that day. But I was never able to vanquish Junior. When he exited our lives eight months later, it wasn't because my dad and I had teamed up to take him down—only that my aunt Carol got a job in Hawaii and they moved away. But well before he left, my fear of him had hardened into hate. True and genuine hate burned inside of me. I don't care what people say about hate, it kept me alive. It saved me from him. He was a tyrant. If I had given in to his way of seeing things, of believing God hated us, that I was an awful, irredeemable person, I'd have been lost. Some unnamable thing inside me knew that, a kind of low-level awareness that allows little kids to survive the world when it's at its ugliest.

I think of my younger self in the living room, biting the heads off fleas and flicking them into the space heater, and I know that I was already a beast by then. The darkness around me, my hatred for Junior, it all coalesced into a stubborn force that kept me half feral. But I knew in my heart it was better to be a beast and live than to try to be good when the rules of being good were meant to kill your soul.

Chapter 8

Garbage Mountain

My mom and Bill had moved across the country and were now living in Waterville, Vermont, in a house that, like all their other houses, sat in the middle of nowhere. When I arrived that summer to stay with them, the grass was blooming like crazy and the pollen made a haze. As a kid from western Washington, thick humidity was new to me and hampered my movements a bit. It wasn't unpleasant. It was a sensation like the air could push in enough to shrink me down into a cozy miniature world too small for the rest of the world to notice.

We quickly slipped into the routine of past summers. My parents worked in Stowe, a little over a forty-minute drive away, and I was left alone during the days. I had soon done everything visible to me: walked the fields being retaken by milkweed and goldenrod, poked around in the old barn, looked in the pond for bullfrogs to catch, paged through my stepdad's archaeology books, played with the two plastic horses I'd stuffed in my suitcase from my dad's house.

Our place was a little run-down two-story farmhouse from the 1800s, with windows filled with the bluest sky at the end of narrow, slanted hallways. The amber wood floors always felt warm. It still held previous tenants' belongings from decades gone by. On the wood pegs on the wall between the garage and kitchen hung numerous coats, most of which were not ours, and that no one would ever come back for—ghosts' coats. We didn't question this or move them, we just lived beside them like it was a normal thing to do. Most were for winter and smelled a little musty, wool plaids and thick felts. In the kitchen were the ghosts' pots and pans.

Along with the everyday items of the ghosts, we also lived with an unholy and huge pile of their garbage in the woodshed garage. Taller than a man, it spread over the main dirt floor and part of a dangerous mezzanine level like a sleeping dragon. The air was thick with stink, as my stepdad had used a BB gun to shoot a jelly jar off a poor skunk who'd gotten his head trapped. The skunk was unharmed but had let loose its signature fury all over the refuse pile. The stink was so *close*! It was as if you had the stench fastened over your mouth and nose like an underwater breathing apparatus in that woodshed.

The humidity made it hard to sleep. It seemed every night at my windowsill massive purple thunderheads gathered and pushed in close but never let loose any rain, just heat lightning. It was beautiful, muted orange, but sticky, and the rumblings of dry thunder were very loud. Crickets and frogs competed with the thunder, which was glorious. One of the things I loved to do was read, but I hadn't brought any books with me. My parents had set up my room and included a kids' illustrated version of *David Copperfield* that someone must have given them, or was maybe left by a ghost. David fucking Copperfield. I was so desperate, I *made* myself read it.

So, maybe a week in, I stood in front of that enormous pile of stinking garbage on a quest. I was going to snoop through the whole thing, by god, and I would find something of interest. I carefully began climbing up its face, my shitty Kmart tennis shoes with blown-out sides slipping wildly. Sharp things poked through my socks. Faded faces of smiling cows and Mrs. Cleaver types gazed up at me from the labels of decades-old jars. About a third of the way up the pile, I was able to see farther back onto the mezzanine, and lo and behold, there were magazines! I *had* to get to them. Around back of the main pile was a rotting loft ladder. I shuffled, slid, and stumbled my way to it over the east slope of Garbage Mountain. Sweet, cloying, skunky excitement filled me up. I had a purpose, and nothing could stop me, not even tetanus. When I reached the back, I saw that the bottom three rungs of the ladder were busted off. I looked around and saw a handle-less pink kid's beach bucket and slid over to retrieve it. I put it under that ladder and wobbled up on it, grabbing the middle rungs with both hands. I clung on and spidered my way up. I'd worry about getting down later.

The air glittered with dust dancing on beams of summer sunlight. No one had been up there in years. There were messy drifts of magazines and newspapers everywhere. Here and there you could see where the floor had rotted away to the main room below. Toward a back wall there was an old brown plastic rocking horse with white socks and a wide blaze and flaring, rosy nostrils, just like the one I used to ride at the horrible nursery school! I was way too old for such things, but I wasn't going to leave the horse up here, unloved and forgotten. It was wired into a pockmarked chrome frame with metal springs. I crabbed along the wall and freed it from its corner with a little effort. I slid it up onto a pile of magazines, centered it like I was using it as a curling stone, and gave it an artful push. It slid down with a soft thud and metallic squeaking. Magazines cascaded down behind it like they'd been poured from a milk pitcher in the sky. I heaved a sigh of accomplishment and gazed down through the hole. More sparkling dust rose to celebrate with me. I remembered I was on a dangerous ledge and backed up a little, uncovering a face that had been obscured by my right shoe. It was Alfred E. Neuman.

This was the first *Mad* magazine I had ever seen. I picked it up and flipped through it quickly. There were cartoons! Most of the other magazines were ag periodicals, and not the good kind with pictures of animals. Leaving those, I chucked the *Mad* magazine down through the hole and made my way back down.

I gathered my treasures and a glass of Kool-Aid lemonade from the 1950s fridge. The house had a glassed-in front porch with a swing made of half a metal bunk bed frame hanging by chains from the ceiling, covered with a bunch of lumpy pillows fashioned from ancient feathers and old overalls. I set up the springy horse next to the swing and got comfortable. My lemonade sweated on an old crate as I settled in to pore over my first-ever *Mad* magazine. It was the October 1972 issue. It was for kids, but it wasn't? It was dark and funny, even though it was ten years old, which, to twelve-year-old me, was ANCIENT.

Over the next few weeks, I read through it hundreds of times. The women in it were all booby nurse stereotypes, but there was Spy vs. Spy, and Al Jaffee's crazy-detailed, surreal drawings. Every part of that issue is tattooed in my brain, and acts like a memory portal to the very slow, beautiful, heavy-scented summer that changed my life for the better, showing me a different, kinder world.

My days flowed by like thick liquid. On one of the rare forays into town with my mom we went into a pet shop to get some dog food. There was a pen of teddy bear hamsters by the front door. They were longhaired and fuzzy, unlike regular hamsters, and I wanted one so bad—*so* bad. There was a special where you could get a hamster, a cage with a built-in wheel, and a first round of food and supplies for one low price.

I immediately started begging.

"You'll need to get a job," my mom said, which she knew full well was impossible. I was twelve, and we lived in deep space as far as jobs were concerned. Her answer wasn't just about not wanting to pay for something I wanted on impulse. Or being tired from work (though she was). I could feel something was changing between us. She used to let me draw close to her at least occasionally, but those moments were now getting farther and farther between. She seemed to want to distance me, like a cat weaning a kitten. It wasn't out in the open, never explicitly spoken, but existed like a charge of negative electricity between us.

I set my jaw in silence. "Oh yeah?"

The next morning, I rustled through the ghosts' things in the empty house after my parents left for work. I found a janky baby stroller near Garbage Mountain and, on one of the pegs in the kitchen, a blue plaid girl's coat with a fake-fur collar and brown fake-leather buckles on the sides. It was still early enough in summer that it was chilly in the morning, and I needed something warm to wear. At least no one lived near me, so I was willing to walk into the world looking like a fashion plate from a decade that only existed on the moon. To add fashion insult to injury, the stroller also had a green plaid pattern on it. I was a Bay City Rollers hobo. I modified the stroller with a bag so my treasure would not fall through the baby leg holes, then I set out to collect garbage from the ditches of the dirt roads. Vermont had a five-cent bounty on cans and bottles, as well as enough good old boys to throw them out the windows of their cars and trucks at high speed.

Hamster money!

I went every morning before the sun got too high.

After a few weeks and a well-timed five-dollar bill from my Gramma Fortini, Bill's mom, I had enough money. I'm sure my mom was pissed, but she and Bill took me to the pet store and I picked out a fuzzy blond hamster and named him Alexander the Great, Alex for short.

Just when I didn't think I could read my *Mad* magazine one more goddamn time on the hot porch, something happened. That night when my parents got home, I met them in the driveway: "What's for dinner!? I'm *hungry*!"

Before they could answer, a wood-paneled station wagon pulled up behind them and the window rolled down. A friendly-looking woman with big glasses said, "Hello! I'm your neighbor, Ilene McDermott, and these are my girls, Annie and Leslie."

Annie was about my age, and she smiled shyly at me from the back seat. She had *thick* curly brown hair and pretty brown eyes. The younger girl, Leslie, was about seven and had long blond hair held in place with plastic barrettes. She waved a little kid wave at me.

My parents and Ilene exchanged a little information about themselves. In Vermont this takes a long time. People love to shoot the shit. I stood shyly behind my parents, not daring to make eye contact with anyone, focusing on the "wood" of the wood paneling on their car.

Then I heard Ilene say, "I heard you had a girl about Annie's age." Turning to me, she said, "You should come down and play with the girls! Do you like horses? We have two."

The girls were silent on the subject.

"OK," I said. I sounded sheepish but inside I was exploding: HORSES! Out of nowhere.

"Wonderful!" Ilene said. "Come by tomorrow!"

So it was settled.

I was *so* nervous and excited as my parents and I went back into the house. Something was happening! Something with *horses*!

The next day I walked the half mile down the dirt road to the McDermotts' house. I was dreading knocking on the door the whole way there, but luckily the whole family was already outside when I arrived, so I got to skip that part.

Their house was a cute two-story log cabin with a matching little barn. As I took it all in, it seemed too good to be true. I was greeted enthusiastically by Ilene, and she introduced me to her husband, Duck. He was a slight man with dark curly hair and a mustache. Then Ilene suggested Annie and I groom her Shetland pony, Gypsy, a dapply, piebald pinto with a fat cream-colored mane and tail.

Annie was soft-spoken and polite. Even though we were both shy, we very quickly burned our way to being best friends—not just because of proximity but out of a real love match. Annie was a genuine and kind kid, and we both wanted to get along without the usual cruelty of childhood I was used to.

The rest of the summer, Annie, her little sister Leslie, me, and my dog Sasha (who refused to stay home) were inseparable. We rode all over the county on Gypsy and Beaver, Annie's mom's quarter horse. We would trade off democratically. We looked hilarious when we were out riding together, as Beaver was a tall horse and Gypsy came up to my twelve-year-old waist. We didn't care; we were in heaven. We groomed Gypsy until she was sleek as an otter.

Annie and I would spend the night at each other's house, and we had a clubhouse in Annie's hayloft, which Sasha the dog even crashed by teaching herself to climb the ladder. We would have to carry her down. We talked about our anticipation of getting our periods and other things girls worry about before they are quite "young adults." We worked on becoming better riders and, with the help of Ilene, we were trying to "train" Gypsy for a horse show. The truth was, Gypsy already knew what she was doing, and also we didn't have a show to go to. Annie and I didn't know exactly what we were "training" her for anyway, but we didn't care.

Every day, I noticed how happy I was, and I knew I didn't want to return to my lonely school in Washington. I loved the weather in Vermont; I loved the trees and the fairy-tale forests. I loved our friendly neighbors, and most of all I loved my new friend and her family and the way they made me feel about myself. I still barely saw my mom and Bill, but Ilene and Duck showed me a tremendous amount of affection and care. I ate dinner with them *a lot*; and Ilene fed me my first-ever fried green tomato. (It was a masterpiece.) They evinced a steady interest in me and what my inner life might include, and as the weeks went on, I could feel myself growing as glossy as Gypsy the pony with the attention. There was hardly any summer left by then, so, summoning the same courage required to ask my dad to turn off the lunatic pastor, I asked my parents to let me stay for the fall semester. They all agreed it was OK. I was over the moon and so was Annie.

We continued the happy routine of our lives but now with extra vigor. One day Ilene said that she had a big announcement. She had signed Annie and me up for a local horse show, called a gymkhana. As equestrian events go, a gymkhana is basically games on horseback, not so much about looking pretty or wearing fancy outfits. It meant a lot of work for Ilene, but she had done it just so her daughter and I could have an experience straight out of a book. I'll never stop loving her and Annie for including me in that.

On the morning of the show, I woke up very early and dressed in my best T-shirt and jeans. I might even have brushed my hair, though I doubt it. What I do remember is I had to lock poor Sasha in the house, saying, "I'm sorry, Sash," through the door as I left. It was still dark as I headed down the hill. The cool morning air cleaned my lungs. I was half walking and half running, dumbstruck with disbelief at my good fortune: I was going to be in a real-life *horse show*! And I would get to *ride*! I was wearing ghost's boots that were too big for me, but I didn't care. *I was gonna ride*. As I approached Annie's, the sun was peeking up over the horizon, spilling an extra magic light over everything. Ilene and Duck were loading tiny Gypsy into the back of their truck, which they had modified into a horse hauler with wooden sides.

I was far too rabid that morning for me to have retained any memory of the ride to the showgrounds. There are just a bunch of joyful, colored smears where that memory should be. We parked the truck and led our sweetheart down the ramp. Annie and I set about grooming her nervously. She was such a kind, willing little horse, and her giving nature gave us confidence. We'd been coached by Ilene, too, about what *not* to do in working with the horses, invaluable lessons in building empathy and awareness for what others may want or need.

During a gymkhana, there are several events throughout the day, and the goal is to accumulate as many points as possible. The points go to the horse, not the rider, so you could ride as a team, which was exactly what Annie and I were. One did not outshine the other. I was to ride the first event, the egg and spoon. I'd have to ride around the arena with an egg balanced on a spoon held in one hand, and then put Gypsy through the paces—walk, trot, canter, reverse direction, etc.—all without dropping the egg. Simple and easy to understand; difficult to execute. I was so nervous and focused on my egg, but I actually ended up winning a scarlet second-place ribbon.

I couldn't focus on the jewel-colored fabric for long because now it was Annie's turn, and as she rode, I could finally take in the arena as a whole. There were horses and ponies of every shape and size *everywhere*. It was just like the 4-H barns at the Northwest Washington Fair, except Annie and I could talk to several of the girls and stroke their horses.

All day, Annie and I switched off riding, taking part in a crazy number of varied events: a timed barrel race, pole bending, halter classes, and relay races. By day's end, we were exhausted and deeply fulfilled. The sweet smell of the horses; my connection to Annie; the kind, watchful eye of Annie's mom; the warm Vermont sunshine—I could feel it all filling me up. I only ended up with a few ribbons, but Annie had a bunch. She was a much better rider than me, but I didn't feel at all bad about it. It was just math.

We were good and tired and ready to go home, but Ilene said it would be a shame to leave without seeing who would win the championship ribbons.

What if we *had won?* she asked.

Wait a sec?

Annie and I hadn't even considered such a possibility. All day, we had been singularly focused on the events at hand; and until that moment, we'd been unaware there was even a final round for points. Could *we* win?

The MC took to the mic and told us we were going to witness the bestowal of third place, then reserve champion, and finally the biggie, grand champion. Third and reserve blew by as Annie's and my nervous stomachs twisted and stretched.

After reserve was awarded, we thought it was *over*. It was even a slight relief accepting we hadn't won. After all, what a day we'd had. Our first horse show! And we had done it as a team.

Then the announcer's voice rose in excitement for the final ribbon, and suddenly he was crowing: "Grand champion, GYPSY."

My knees went soft. Annie whooped, and I whooped, and we hugged hard and jumped up and down like lunatics. Ilene motioned Annie out into the ring with Gypsy to accept her ribbon. Annie stumbled out and people cheered. That purple and yellow and cream ribbon was half as tall as Gypsy herself, and it danced alongside her mane as Annie and Gypsy trotted back to us, their thick hair bobbing in unison, in stunned disbelief. It was (and remains) one of the best days of my life. Ilene had shown so much love and respect and belief in us that we had believed we could triumph, too. This was how the world could be when someone really loved you.

One afternoon that fall, I'd come home from school and gone up to my room. I heard a truck pull up in the driveway. My parents were already home, so I looked out the window. There was a maroon pickup I didn't recognize, with something woolly in the bed, but I couldn't quite make it out.

I went downstairs and could hear my parents speaking seriously with someone. Through a crack in the kitchen door, I saw a man with white hair and a mustache. He looked grim and left in a hurry. When I went in the kitchen, my mom and Bill were clearly shaken.

"What is it?"

Bill told me that our dog Bubba, the big malamute, had been accused of killing one of the neighbor's sheep.

That's what that woolly lump had been. I felt sick.

"Well, he didn't do it!!" I yelled.

"He did," Bill said softly. "Mr. Bruce saw him."

I knew in my heart he was right, but I didn't want to accept it. We had had Bubba since we lived on the Colville reservation, and he was the most gentle and loving dog. At least to people. He and I would sing together in the daytime. He was easy to get howling—he loved to do it—and when he really got going he'd sound like he was talking. He hated it in the house, so we would keep him on a long chain by his doghouse during the day, then let him off the chain to go run with Sasha at dusk. The two of them would always come back within the hour and he would come right over and let you snap the chain on his collar, panting and wagging his tail. Mr. Bruce had given Bill the choice of either killing Bubba or paying for the sheep. We had no money for sheep. Bill felt terrible about what Bubba had done, even though he was just being true to his nature. Bill had found him running with coyotes on the reservation, after all. It was settled. Bubba was to die the next day. Bill would take him to his friend's house in the morning, who would do it as a favor. There was no way Bill could have pulled the trigger. He loved that dog too much.

I just couldn't believe it. This perfectly healthy dog was going to die. Why couldn't we just give him to someone else? Bill explained that it wouldn't be right, and he needed to do the honorable thing, even though it was the worst thing. I cried most of the night. The next morning, I said goodbye to Bubba with shuddering sobs. My mom and Bill put him in the car and drove away. I had a half hour till the school bus came, so I sat by the woodstove and cried.

The high of the horse show and the low of Bubba's death mingled in me.

School was a whirl of happiness, though, unlike anything I had previously experienced. Everyone there was poor and wearing hand-me-downs, so no one talked about each other's clothes or singled each other out for ridicule. I made friends. I could crest along, feeling like one in a gang. But no matter how happy I was, I knew time was running out, and I'd have to return to Washington at the winter break. The semester was going to end with a big holiday Christmas pageant, and we got to vote on its theme. It was "Space" by a landslide. I was required to make a Martian costume, and I thrilled at the opportunity. I asked my mom to help, and she flaccidly agreed. She was tired. Our car was busted, and she and my stepdad had to hitchhike into Stowe to work. My mom had been harassed by someone while out on the road and was still shaken by whatever had happened. This is where my step-dad's shortcomings were; he was a wonderful guy, but lacked empathy for the vulnerability my mother experienced that he didn't as a man. She was exhausted from work, not happy in general—and I could feel that charge of negative electricity between us pulsing. I could feel her pushing me away. She told me we had no money to buy costume stuff. But I was not gonna give in.

"C'mon, there's got to be *something*!" I said. "Can't I at least get some tinfoil!?"

Nope.

She suggested we look through the ghosts' things, but there was nothing to make a space costume out of. There wasn't even anything green for a Martian outfit! I began to cry. How could we *be* so poor? How could my parents let me down like this? For the first time, I felt part of a community that expected something from me, and I was going to fail.

My mom started a sullen, sarcastic tirade about how maybe she should be more like Ilene McDermott: "Oh, she's the *perfect* mother! Well, I'm sooooo sorry I'm not her..." Blah, blah, blah. I shut down. Later, my stepdad came into my room where I was pouting and told me I'd hurt my mother's feelings.

In the end, all the ghosts could provide was a huge soccer hooligan shirt from the sixties with a green stripe across the front, and so that's what I wore. I skulked through the pageant like a wet, gray mop. I was still a kid, of course—mortified not to have a costume, and powerless, too, to express the larger disappointments of my situation. Deep down I knew that while my mom might have said otherwise, she wasn't jealous of where my affections went. Not really. Likewise, I knew her exhaustion wasn't just with work and winter. It was with me—not just as a kid asking for a costume, but as a kid attached to her by a long, ratty kite string she wanted to snip. This was the struggle that had been between us forever, and in the past I had responded by making myself as quiet and obedient as I could. If a rattlesnake had bitten me to death the summer we lived on the Colville reservation, I would have arranged myself to die in an angel's shape, all to make her love me. But now I was starting to push back—to shout at what wasn't fair, even when I wasn't quite sure what to shout. At least part of what emboldened me was the kindness I'd experienced with Annie's family. I now knew that a gentler way of being existed, and that knowledge mixed with my defiance. It was as if Garbage Mountain, this pile of unwanted things, started shaking itself to life.

Chapter 9

Scum with a Bad Perm

I feel so fortunate that my first kiss was a good one. It was the spring semester of sixth grade, and there was a new boy in school named Lonnie. He was a gangly kid with buck teeth, big swimmy eyes, and curly, straw-colored hair. My friends and I were bored, and he came along right when we needed him. We peeked at him and giggled and whispered. I don't know where the idea came from that I should kiss the new kid after school; it was probably started on a note where you had to check a box. I'm sure I didn't suggest it to him myself, but somehow it was arranged. The note network got shit *done*. So it was settled: After school I would meet him by the track and kiss him, more of a dare than an expression of interest.

That day we were both wearing our super-tough John Rogers Elementary Seagulls PE shirts. Lonnie was a tall kid, unusual for boys our age. As we approached each other, I just kept getting shorter. My heart was pounding. I had to get this over with. The pressure was killing me! I was simultaneously thrilled because I was doing something prohibited, a thrill I would savor more and more in years to come. I dared not look him in the face, that was far too embarrassing.

"OK, NOW!"

I pulled the trigger in my mind and launched upward at him as he came toward me. Since I also had buck teeth and my aim was bad, we essentially clashed our enamel together. *BAM.* It hurt. It was like a fight between two rabbits that was over *really* quickly. We were laughing, and my friends were laughing, but I broke to lope off, grab my stuff, and go home, too stunned to engage any further.

The next day the word on the street was that he and I were now "going together." That was news to me, but OK. We would consciously avoid each other unless we fell into talking naturally in a group. A few days later my friend Tomi told me she would also like to "go with him." I was a little shocked, but immediately relented. Tomi was another horse girl; she had gorgeous thick black hair and liked country music. She was awesome and straightforward, so why not?

This period we were sailing through was, I recognize now, the tail end of innocence. The end of our kinder climate. Embedded in the word "kinder" is the word "kind." It's from the old Germanic "Kundjaz," meaning "family." And of course, even in modern German, "Kinder" means "children." In old English, "(ge)cynde" meant nature, the natural order, related to kin, etc. I love to think that these old languages were instilling the idea that "*kind*ness" should be our basic state of existence; of being family with all mankind, that mankind is capable of being the gorgeous, tender beast I believe deep down we can be.

Not long after my kiss with Lonnie, our class was sitting through a rained-in recess. Rain slapped against the windows. The overhead lights buzzed the soundtrack to our doldrums. This was the fourth recess in a row that had been canceled, and we sat miserably at our desks under orders to "amuse ourselves quietly." Then someone got an idea.

Rudy was a big, smart, and funny Indigenous kid who absolutely *loved* AC/DC. That day, under Rudy's direction, an indestructible record player was brought from the AV room and we were off to the races. Rudy had brought *Back in Black* to school. He dropped the heavy stylus on side B, where the album's title track sat. A powerful pressure built up in my chest with the first hammerhead creeper notes of the song. Even through the nasal compression caused by the school record player, the energy could not be dimmed. I was too shy to dance around, and it was sublime torture to sit still. My foot started to tap and tap some more. It might not have looked like much from the outside, but inside it felt like I had turned into an electrical transformer—showering sparks as the lyrics snaked through the room. My dad was into rock, but AC/DC was not on his radar. They were a little too raw. This music, this feeling, was going to be MINE, *all* mine—I just knew it.

In the row next to me, Jamie, Rudy's best friend, had crawled under his desk and was head-banging, giggling like a fool. Rudy, having completed his recess rescue mission, had gone back to drawing something complicated at his desk, an easy smile on his face.

As I listened, I thought, *What if we could all just stay together like this? Not just this year but into junior high?* I wanted that to be possible. I hoped it would be.

Guess what?

It wasn't.

As I moved through puberty, a part of me felt betrayed by my own biology—why did I have to be attracted to *boys*? To other human bodies at all? The increasing distraction in me—who did I think was cute, who might I want to kiss?—felt like some sort of treachery emanating from within my own body. I'd always loved horses so sincerely, and now there was this pressure, not just from the world but from inside *me*, to transfer my attention. I trusted animals so much more than people—I wanted only to love them. When it came to liking another human, I was perplexed as to why I would want to give my attention to something so unknown, so unpredictable.

I looked like a little kid longer than the other kids, a narrow-hipped child with no boobs and so no excuse to wear a bra. I was awkward as a baby mule, all knees, even where my elbows should be. After gym, all the girls would have to be naked together in the locker room, and I could see the difference between my body and theirs.

I was behind in other ways, too. One weekend, a girl named Beth, who I had been in grade school with before she changed schools, invited me to a party at her house, which was in a sparkly new development of cookie-cutter houses next to a copse of trees that had until recently been part of a complete forest. The trees still looked stunned and traumatized by what had happened. The party was held in the backyard of the house, and whenever I felt especially out of place I'd go off on my own to look around the neighboring woodlet. While I was roaming there, a dark tabby kitten darted out of the underbrush and began to rub against my pant legs, mewing. It followed me back to the party. The other girls seemed out of my league; they didn't care about things like kittens. They liked boys and important things. I'd orbit the fringes of their conversations, listening, then wander off to look around some more, the kitten at my heels.

At some point I found a huge moth that looked just like a leaf. Such a beauty! Such genius camouflage. I couldn't believe my luck. What were the odds of even *finding* such a miraculous creature? I had only ever seen anything like it in *National Geographic*. I located a Dixie cup and put the moth inside, lightly covering it with a napkin. I wanted to show my dad, who I thought would be impressed. I was still always trying to wave down his attention, even if it never really worked. By then, the sun was getting low, and we were all ushered inside to have cake and see Beth's new purplish-pink bedroom. We were all admiring it when my moth got out and flew up and landed on some matching pink Levolor blinds.

To my embarrassment, and the other girls' horror, the moth began to lay large green eggs on the blinds.

"Oh my GOD!!!" Beth yelled. "Get that thing out of here!"

I went back outside and let the moth go. It seemed raggedy and tired as it flew away. I felt so terrible. Then I heard a little mewing coming from a newly planted cookie-cutter bush. I would end up taking the kitten home that day. In the car, the joy of her warm purring presence against my chest was set against the cold, certain knowledge that Beth was going to dump me after this. I understood it. She wanted to be a cheer-leader, and someone like me, boobless and in ratty no-name jeans, was only going to drag her down. I was the green moth eggs on her pink blinds.

There were forces in play here—for Beth, for me—that went beyond a single friendship. In my case, without ever thinking about it much, I'd enjoyed a largely gender-free exis-tence across childhood. It suited me. When I was with my cousins Brent and Jay, the marker of difference between us was that I was the oldest, not that I was a girl. I liked jeans with trucks on the pockets; I would have slept in a stable as just one of the horses if I could have. Though I had warm feelings about Shaun Cassidy *and* Jodie Foster as a kid, that wasn't just about attraction. It was about a desire to roam the world with-out constriction. But now, as I became a teenager, I was going to become a girl in a way I hadn't ever been before. It wasn't even a conscious choice—it was simply me breathing in the atmosphere around me, the same as Beth was. She had just arrived there sooner.

Boys in bands would replace horses in my daydreams and conversation: musicians like Nick Rhodes of Duran Duran, Adam Ant, and Joan Jett, resplendent with their dark eyeliner and bright leathers. It was like the gods of my own private mythology got jostled away from me. On some level, I resented the boys in bands even as I hung their posters. I thought it was because they had usurped the rightful place of my main, loyally held passion, but what's obvious now is that I wanted to *be* the boy in the band and just didn't have a way of acknowledging it. My desire, still mysterious to me, was to live in a world where my old gods, like horses and moths, and my new gods of music could coexist, in a pantheon. But such a world didn't exist, and the pull to be "a girl" was too strong. I couldn't not do it. And in becoming one, I abandoned the gods of my childhood and so, for a long time, broke my own heart.

I walked the halls at school trying to shiver myself out of anyone's notice, so they wouldn't make fun of my Kmart clothes or the new puffy perm I'd gotten, which I'd hoped would be cool but had only made me more of a target for ridicule. There were other shunned kids at school, and we could have been friends with each other, but the social rules were so harsh, we were afraid the other spurned kids might rub off on us. It was understood between us, like a code, and so none of us took it personally when even the other shunned kids gave us a wide berth. Maybe we all still clung to some delusion that we were good enough—even if just barely!—to keep out of reach of being totally unacceptable? We had to think that way; what other choice did we have? And so we orbited each other at a distance, like magnets pushing each other away.

There were a couple of boys who liked to pick on me and a few other girls in the lunchroom. They represented the essential hormonal shift into human cruelty. I no longer remember their names, but one was the despicably ugly-souled "hot guy" and the other was his toadie, who believed he was hot by proxy. The leader had blond hair and Nicolas Cage eyebrows, so I shall refer to them here, respectively, as Eyebrows and the Turd. One day we had cinnamon rolls for dessert with lunch, a rare and awesome treat. I was so hungry and life was so dismal, I'd latch on to *anything* even remotely good, like a desperate turtle trying to keep my little pinhole nostrils above the surface in a garbage aquarium. A cinnamon roll for dessert was that kind of happy thing. It sat on the tray in front of me, fat as an ottoman with the white frosting gleaming like snow.

Eyebrows and the Turd were swanning around the cafeteria and I saw them notice that I still hadn't eaten my dessert.

Fuckkkkkk! my brain screamed. But it was too late. They were sitting down across from me.

"Hey, baby," sleazed Eyebrows. "Can I have your cinnamon roll? Please, cutie? You can be my girlfriend?"

I was so angry and degraded that I was being forced to play along with this. I couldn't say a word.

"Cmon, baby." The Turd smirked, showing yellow teeth.

I sat, all of my muscles clenched. Then Eyebrows reached across the table and began touching my cinnamon roll. I cracked. Without a word, I dumped what was left on my tray in his lap, then stood and began to walk away.

The Turd's gasp was followed by a "You fucking BITCH!" from Eyebrows.

My cinnamon roll was gone, and there wasn't even a crowd to applaud my rebellion.

Luckily, after some time—and after getting the rest of my perm cut out—I managed to make a couple of great friends. One was a rocker chick named Alicia, and another was Katrina, who was into volleyball. They both liked MTV, too, and that was my in. We wrote each other notes in rainbow colors about the bands we liked and the teachers we didn't. We stayed over at each other's house and watched *Saturday Night*

Live so we could catch Eddie Murphy's newest skit. We laughed a lot, the three of us, and I knew I never wanted it to stop because that other stuff couldn't touch me as long as the three of us were laughing together.

At home, my aunt and uncle hadn't left for Hawaii yet, and my dad's Bible reading and the playing of fire-and-brimstone sermons and discussions with them about Satan walking as a real beast "right here among us" continued.

I had to go to Saturday school, which I *hated*. We sat in a circle on chairs in the church basement while the youth pastor, who looked like a boiled hot dog in a turtleneck, gently told us why we were all going to hell, which was right beneath us. I seethed. The day he went for music, I might have exploded had it not been for a kid named Matt.

I didn't know a single one of these kids at "youth group" and didn't want to. We were all there against our will, and that made us off limits to each other somehow, like we were being held hostage. On this particular day, the youth pastor was explaining how the music we liked on the radio was indeed satanic.

Some redheaded kid blurted, "I'm sorry, even Hall and Oates?"

Yep, them too.

Then this kid Matt piped up. He was about fourteen or so, a little older than me, with brown hair that went to his ears, which was "long" to church people. He was tall and wearing a nice flannel shirt and I could see a Def Leppard T-shirt just barely peeking out above the second button from the top.

Matt proceeded to very civilly argue with the youth pastor that his favorite band, Def Leppard, was *not* satanic.

He brought up their song "Photograph."

"The song isn't about Satan, man, it's about love," reasoned Matt.

"Love is not venal, Matthew."

"Vee-null??" Matt, puzzled, screwed up his face a little. "He's looking at a *photo*, man! And missing her *respectfully*! How is that possibly satanic?" He extended his hands in the "why" position.

The English band Def Leppard were around making radio hits and soft-focus fog machine videos throughout the eighties. After the monolithic music producer Mutt Lange worked with powerhouse bands like AC/DC, he went on to make genetically engineered pop music. Def Leppard was one of those projects. Laughably marketed as "heavy metal" and "hard rock," they had so far done nothing to endear themselves to thirteen-year-old me. I was a full-fledged music snob by then. I referred to Def Leppard and their ilk as "Pussy Metal."

The idea that Def Leppard might be satanic was truly laughable. If they had been, it would have been a satanism so harmless they might as well have been Bing Crosby singing "Silver Bells." But Matt's passion and conviction that there was nothing harmful about listening to their records or wearing a T-shirt with their name on it *did* carve a warm place for Def Leppard in my heart.

That night, bolstered by Matt's protest, I nervously told my dad I didn't want to attend church anymore. What was nuts is that he said "OK," very softly, and didn't try to convince me to stay.

I stood in disbelief, glad but wary. *Why was that so easy? Was it a trap?* It wasn't a trap, but instead, as I would learn many years later, a footprint left from a dark period in my dad's past. His quiet acquiescence was a clue left on the ground, a key to why he always kept me at arm's distance, but it was one I wouldn't be able to decipher for a long time.

Chapter 10

Rock Show

One Friday night, all of us were out on the Ave in Seattle, and it was getting late. My friend Petra and I were hanging out with some goth kids and having a good time. The streetlights turned the seasonal mist sparkly and the neon shop windows glowed, their warmth filling my chest with a peculiar longing. It seemed like we were almost always on the cold side of those windows.

I was fourteen, and music had bloomed into a full-time obsession. I really loved the Seattle radio stations KJET and KCMU, with C89.5 an occasional visit for dance music. Between the two K stations there was every kind of independent, experimental, punk, new wave, and goth music from all over the world. It was heaven. I still liked Top 40 music, too, but that wouldn't last long. There was just too much to choose from. I also loved MTV and especially *Night Flight*, a cable show that would show videos and rock and roll movies. *Ladies and Gentlemen, the Fabulous Stains* blew my mind right out the back of my skull. All I wanted was music. I was wracked with it—it animated all my movements. I even tried to convey music in my awkward fashion style. Ripped jeans with dark nylons underneath. Cat-eye makeup in bold colors, teased-up hair, and homemade chunky jewelry. I had a cross earring that I fashioned out of two pieces of broken compact mirror. Many people coveted that earring, but especially my friend Petra. I was kinda femme but also tried to project the toughness inside me, to no avail. I pierced my own nose and was *dying* for a leather jacket. I was too poor, though.

Petra and I met in art class. She was bold and loud, and she had decided in her winning, bossy way that I was going to be her friend. She had a very long Mohawk and a million piercings. We talked about music all the time. We would laugh ourselves sick watching horror movies like *C.H.U.D.* and *Maniac Cop*, and talked late into the night. We started making a couple of other friends in our art class and soon managed to rack up a sort of a social currency, weak as it was. There were a couple of junior girls who were into new wave. They hung out with college kids outside of school, and I thought they were so sleek and adult. I struck up a friendship with one, Carrie Elfman. She took a sort of sisterly interest in me and even loaned me her Nina Hagen twelve-inch of "New York, New York." I took it home and devoured it over the weekend. I had never held anything so precious in my hands. I couldn't believe such a cool girl would loan *me* her record. It felt like we'd passed a friendship threshold; we weren't as tight as I was with Petra, but it was a significant bond.

Carrie's brother Bryce was nineteen, and I met him once when he picked her up from school. He was handsome and friendly in a way I found flattering. They were older and could drive and so went to rock shows and dance clubs like Skoochies or the Monastery (which Petra and I could *never* get into at fourteen). Undeterred, Petra and I decided we were gonna go meet like-minded punks in the U District and Capitol Hill on our own. Partly because Petra had a new Mohawk to show off and partly because we were hungry for music! We'd take the bus for what seemed *hours* on the weekend from Mountlake Terrace to Seattle and wander around. We had virtually no money. We would go to record stores and buy nothing, grab copies of *The Rocket*, and get a coffee at McDonald's just to get out of the rain. We met a lot of goth kids and a couple of punks, including a guy named Mike from Alaska. Mike had eyes like a husky, so blue they were almost white, and he knew more about underground music than anyone I'd ever met. Many people were rigid in what they would admit to liking, but not Mike. He gave me a mixtape that would shape my future. The bands blew my mind: Psi Com, Danielle Dax, the Butthole Surfers, Wolfgang Press, Psychic TV, Big Black, Effigies, Exhumed, Corrosion of Conformity, Celtic Frost, and the Avengers, among others.

Our little group was gathered on the sidewalk when I saw a familiar face coming toward us. It was Carrie's brother Bryce.

"What are you guys up to?"

I explained we were hanging out but would be going home soon.

"You need a ride?" he asked. "I'm headed back."

I couldn't believe this good fortune. Petra could stay out later with her goth pals and I would get a ride home from a handsome guy, the brother of my cool new friend.

We said goodbye and headed down the Ave. At some point he turned and picked me up and set me on the lip of a pay phone and kissed me. I was blown away: All this and he *likes* me!? I was electrified, trembling, hovering above us, already imagining telling the story to Petra. I had never been kissed by a full-grown man before, just a couple of boys on the brink of discovering they were very gay. Not that I would ever have traded those kisses for the world; I was honored that they felt safe and trusted me. Still, this was just *different*. We walked until we found his car, a blue MG. I felt like a movie star as I got in; he even held the door for me. It was raining as usual and the streetlights dancing on the black street looked extra beautiful.

About halfway home, he asked if it was cool if we stopped by his place quickly.

"Sure," I said.

This is when it turned. He raped me. He was nineteen. I was fourteen. I had gotten my first period two weeks before. Afterward, he dumped me off at home with barely a quick "goodbye" and drove off.

When I got home that night I was in trouble. I was late, having taken advantage of the fact that my Gramma Case was staying to watch me while my dad was out of town. With a sad look on her face, she informed me that she would have to tell him how I had disrespected her. I listened, then went to my room.

Petra called the next day. She had gone to see *Rocky Horror* with the goth kids.

"Did anything happen with Bryce?" she asked.

"Yep," I said, quickly and ashamedly.

"Well," she said. "You got it over with."

When she said that, I had a funny feeling, not relief exactly but something close. I had never had any solid idea what "it" was *supposed* to be, and at least "it" wasn't a mystery anymore. "It," it turned out, wasn't special. In fact, "it" sucked. That this "it" had been horribly disappointing because it was rape was something I wasn't yet willing to consider. My body was already burying that fact as fast as my hind legs could dig. Petra didn't probe, but I felt an unspoken tenderness between us.

When my dad got home, I was grounded for a month. I didn't care. I felt like such a fool. I couldn't believe I had been so stupid. I was just relieved he didn't know what happened, which, in my mind, had already become entirely my fault.

That Monday, I took Carrie's Nina Hagen record to school to give back to her.

I could see from her face that she wasn't happy to see me.

"Hi," I said.

She took the record without a look or word of acknowledgment and just kept speaking to her friend. "I told him to stay away from idiot young girls…"

I blacked the rest out, I was so stunned. Feeling sick, I crawled off to art class, where I told Petra what happened.

"Fuck her!" she said. Thank god for Petra. I don't know what I would have done without her.

Over the next month I withdrew into music and just kept my head down. One day, after I was no longer grounded, Petra decided that we should go see D.O.A., Nomeansno, the Fastbacks, and the Accüsed at Gorilla Gardens, an all-ages club by the train station. She had the genius idea that we would tell our parents we were going to a dance at Shoreline High that by lucky coincidence was the same night as the show. Petra's mom would drop us off at the front door of the school, and we would duck around back to meet some friends and get a ride downtown. Little did we know there would be chaperones on the front porch of the high school. As we got out of Petra's mom's car, we saw the human roadblock. Turning, we realized that Petra's mom wasn't planning on leaving until she saw us safely inside.

"GOOOOO!" Petra yelled in a panicky charge. She was a natural leader, and I bolted with her, running around to the back of the school. Thank god the two guys picking us up, who were friends of Petra's brother, were waiting, as planned. We leapt into their little brown car and they floored it. We were so exhilarated that we had ditched Petra's mom and were now on our way to a *real* punk rock show! The guys were just giving us a lift and *not* trying to get in our pants. We were all there for one thing: music. The only thing on earth that never let me down.

Gorilla Gardens was comprised of two theaters: the Gorilla Room and the Omni Room. D.O.A. and the Fastbacks were in the Gorilla, and Nomeansno and the Accüsed were in the Omni. They staggered the show so you could see all the bands in an alternating pattern, which was quite genius. The air was thick with cigarette smoke (clove and regular), sweat, mildew, and stale beer. I felt so high on the throng of sights and smells, stirred up in the way I used to get at the county fair. I noticed every T-shirt, every pin and patch, every hairstyle, every pierced earlobe, every tattoo. It all looked like the freedom I so desperately wanted. I was a little human mansion with all the windows thrown open to let the air in, my curtains billowing and whirling.

At the Omni, the first band I remember was the Accüsed. They were four metal-looking guys with very messy hair. Blaine, the sweaty, shirtless singer, started the crowd favorite "Martha Splatterhead" and people went wild. The music physically pushed me in a way it did not coming through my radio. It taunted and throbbed and I did, too, with a kind of urgent electricity. Next, we headed over to the Gorilla to see the Fastbacks. I was so shocked to see two women onstage playing guitar and bass! I had never really thought about women playing guitars, but Lulu and Kim made me immediately realize my failure of imagination. I remember Kurt Bloch and one other person onstage—maybe it was when Duff McKagan from Guns N' Roses was briefly in the band? That's likely wishful thinking, but I'll allow it. I remember Lulu taking no shit from lippy, misogynist audience members, shutting them down before they were even finished with their flaccid bullshit. Petra and I swooned.

Next up was Nomeansno, who had driven down from

Victoria in British Columbia. Musically they hit me the hardest. I was mesmerized by Andy Kerr and his frenetic explosions. He looked like a nerdy accountant but tore it the fuck up, the music smart and even melodic. I would love them for a very long time, and I recognized a few of the songs they played that night on their *Sex Mad* album when it came out.

Back in the Gorilla Room, D.O.A. from Vancouver, BC, took the stage. Joey Shithead fired up a chain saw and announced, "I'll be your fire marshal for this evening!" Everyone went crazy. I loved everything about that night: the music, the energy, the people, the anger, the freedom. Petra and I knew we were where we belonged. We didn't want to be popular or get laid or get good grades; we wanted to see live music every night of our lives, forever.

When I got home that night my dad was waiting for me. Petra's mom had called and told him what we had done. "DAD! We just wanted to see *music*!" I said, but it didn't work. I was grounded for another month. I didn't care. I took my punishment with dignity. It was so worth it.

No regrets.

I was set to spend the summer before my sophomore year with my mom and Bill, who had moved back to Washington from the East Coast. What I didn't know then was that it would end up being for what remained of high school. My dad got a job in Alaska working for Exxon as a draftsman, and by the end of that summer, he'd moved as far north as he could, to live on a little spit of land called Point Barrow. My dad seemed happy to go. I think he thought he was going to get rich. Visiting was never mentioned, and whenever I tried to imagine his life there, all I could envision was him walking from one white trailer building to another identical one, connected by some sort of giant hair-dryer hose so his eyes wouldn't freeze. Back and forth, day after day, like a hamster.

Chapter 11

Girls Do That

My dad and I had moved several times over the past few years, and so had my mom and Bill. First to Massachusetts, to be closer to where my Fortini grandparents lived, and then a couple of other places before returning to Washington. They'd settled in the town of Olalla, in a semi-rural spot tucked down a little lane. It was a tiny blue single-story rectangle of a house. My mom had made it very cozy inside, with that gift she had for making dingy places look charming. She had a waitressing job and a car (thank goodness), and a friend had connected Bill with a job somewhere. They were both gone all day, as usual.

I begged to buy fashion magazines to pass the time. I listened to music, especially mixtapes I'd gotten from my friend Mike. I raked the yard. I drew pictures. I did my makeup over and over. I looked at my body in the mirror. It was changing but just so slowly. I had no sense of myself whatsoever. I was the inside of a chrysalis, a murky liquid, viscous lymph and blood. Some dark magic was twisting me. My leg bones hurt all the time.

I scoured the cupboards for something salty or sweet enough to catch my attention, my teenage mouth craving fluorescent food. I practiced shaving my armpits and legs but I had hardly any hair, so it was hard to tell the difference. I had found a book about yoga in the house and would faithfully work through different poses every night just in case I ever became a model—that wasn't going to happen, but the "girls do that" programming that seized my system was now lit up and flashing with the urgency of an answering machine message. At night I *lived* for David Letterman, a bright culture doorway for me to crawl through weeknights at eleven thirty. Mostly, though, I longed. Time was broken, leaving me sullen and withdrawn. I was too cool for my old life, but my new life hadn't arrived yet, trapping me in some kind of hermetically sealed waiting room.

One day, I decided to start tanning, for no other reason than I was bored and "girls do that." Because we had no lawn furniture, I spread a blanket over the bleached grass rectangle above the septic tank and plopped a pillow down, returning inside to gather up a few of the magazines I'd already read ten thousand times so I could read them again. Instead of a swimsuit, I had on a T-shirt with the neck and sleeves cut out and a pair of ill-fitting bike shorts. I arranged my limbs for the sun—a pale wraith of a punk kid with dyed black hair trying to get a tan. I revisited the glossy spreads I'd seen of girls smiling on bikes, girls smiling up at boys, girls smiling as they twirled. Ten minutes had passed, and I raised the hem of my shorts to see if any tan had happened yet. Nope. I sank back against the ground, the summer-dry grass crunching beneath the blanket. Overhead, the sky had the same white-hot look it had back in the summers I'd run around the fair with my cousins. But I saw the sky's expanse differently now. It was the eighties, and the USSR, with all its nuclear weapons, was something we were taught to fear. As I inspected the sky, I couldn't see any silver space stations, but I could feel their lurking presence. I raised my hand and flipped off one of the clouds, in case any Russians were peeking through. Another ten minutes passed, and I retreated into the house, not golden but red and blotchy. No one, I feared, was going to pick me to strike a dramatic flaring-nostril pose in a magazine.

When I'd first arrived in Olalla, I was excited to be reunited with my mom and Bill, but after only a few days it was clear the negative charge between me and my mom crackled stronger than ever. Not the normal bickering push-pull of parent and teenager—this was something more fundamental, something atomized in the air. If I came into a room, I could tell my presence chafed her. Her eyes would look me over from the corner of her lids, and she clearly didn't like what she saw. She began to punish me for the most minor of infractions. When I was a child, I'd seen flares of another her, more rage-filled than the smiling woman she appeared on the surface, and it was like this other her was now seeping through the bars of the cage where she'd been kept.

She started to come home drunk—really, really drunk, like some roadkill reanimated by an evil force. She would drag herself around the house, saying mean and crude things or making up lies. There was something intentional about her cruelty. She didn't want to just disappear, but actively destroy the scaffolding of our love for her as she went. On those nights, my entire body would become hypervigilant as fight-or-flight antifreeze flowed through my veins just from being in the same house as her. Bill was miserable, too, one night growing so frustrated he put her in the shower and turned on the cold water. He thought that would sober her up, but she just looked tiny and drowned and humiliated.

My sophomore year of high school, she and Bill divorced, and with my dad in Alaska, that left her and me together.

I'd become friends with a terrifyingly smart guy named Dean, and we dated for about five seconds. He was the first boy I ever slept with, really, but I don't retain any sentimental memories of the relationship. We were just two teenagers riding their ping-ponging hormones who felt safe enough in each other's company to have sex. But what did I know? I was fifteen, so young and inexperienced that I still thought of being raped as my "first time." After we broke up, we remained part of the same group, the only kids at our rural school to listen to alternative records and hungry enough to go see punk rock music in faraway Seattle.

No adult monitored me anymore, and I began staying out whenever I could. Those nights! They sometimes had a scavenged sort of beauty, but they were awful, too.

Sleeping on floors at depressing parties. Throwing up in sinks next to people's dirty dishes, and waking up on strange musty couches. The different highs of various drugs: the soft loving embrace of MDA, the hyper-focused, surreal, speedy thrill of LSD, the drunk Dr. Seuss world of PCP. I was often hungover from these substances, and they all caused the *worst* hangovers. My spine felt dried out, and I was just an exhausted piece of beef jerky. I was only fifteen. I drank whatever everyone else was drinking. I smoked weed and sniffed poppers, spending many a weekend night sitting uncomfortably in the front seat of someone's car listening to friends do "love shit" in the back seat.

The air quivered and shifted with rotating casts of people, some of them friends, some of them enemies, some just acquaintances sliding by. There were Nazi assholes, and then the people who beat them up. There were sweet people like my friend Rae and her brother Richard, a rocker guy whose car horn played the main riff from "Iron Man." Or these two girls, Deedee and Destiny, one goth, the other straight looking, who traveled everywhere together being an aggressively "erotic" duo. There was Marcus Galang, the metal drummer from Guam, maybe the nicest guy in Port Orchard. His best friend was Kurt, and we would hang at his house in the basement family room, coming down off drugs and watching movies. Kurt had a German shepherd named Caesar who would do the funniest trick I'd ever seen: Kurt would hold a Dorito in his clenched butt cheeks (*over* his pants) and Caesar would appear to eat it out of his ass. We would all be cry-laughing on the floor.

It was not always bad, in other words. But there were times I'd realize that if I disappeared, it was possible no one would notice. And the Green River Killer was always near. I was numb enough to stop being afraid.

I still thought of Bill as my stepdad even though he and my mom had divorced, and he seemed to feel the same way about me, like we were permanently family. One night, he took me out for a meal somewhere. I had probably just recited some infuriating thing my mom had done when Bill told me something so huge my sixteen-year-old brain couldn't even begin to digest it: He said that when my mom was a kid, doing chores at the farm along with her siblings, she'd been kicked in the knee by one of the cows in the barn. Cows are powerful animals. I've since been injured several times by creatures that weigh over fifteen hundred pounds, and it's the kind of thing that gives you a real punching reminder of your mortality, of just how brittle and fragile you are. I have no doubt the kick felt like lightning. My mom had cried—then refused to do any more milking, because she was in pain and scared.

And so, to punish her, her dad had raped her, right there in the barn.

Was it true? I didn't know. When I heard it I thought back to the friendly old man I'd met once when I was little, sitting in his chair and giving me fifty bucks as I left. And I remembered how he was almost never spoken of around my Gramma Mary Ann's house, and how on the rare occasions when he was mentioned, it was in the context of some sort of violence, like how he'd hit my grandmother when they were married. I didn't know what to make of this story. It rumbled through my sixteen-year-old self, its own kind of rampaging animal. I felt great sadness for the little girl Bill was describing, but that girl seemed wholly disconnected from the woman I was living with, who dragged herself through the house drunk as I darted back into my room to lie on the bed, putting the headphones of my crappy Walkman on. The last thing Bill had said about it haunted me: *You look so much like her then, you remind her...* Some snap of understanding came then about why it seemed to bother her to even look at me.

My mom was drinking so heavily that she often forgot to let me in the house. The only time she wasn't out carousing was when she went through a bout of life-threatening pneumonia after falling off a boat while wasted. A friend of hers from the restaurant named Melba, an older woman with permed hair and a beautiful smile, would sometimes bring us groceries. One night when my mom had locked me out, I had to go to the pay phone in our dark little apartment complex and place a collect call to Melba. She came ten minutes later and brought me home to her house. It was so clean, so nice—Melba and her husband quietly moving around its tidy rooms.

That night was one of the last times I'd see Melba, which is something I'm still sorry about. When you're scrambling to survive, you lose bad people—I would eventually lose my mom—but you also lose the good ones like Melba, through no fault of their own. It's the tall wake of your flight that makes it impossible for them to keep you in sight.

By the end of my sophomore year of high school, things had gotten so bad that I asked my mom for an emancipation. I knew a couple of other kids who'd gotten them. She couldn't sign it quickly enough; she didn't even have to think it over.

I was now a "free adult"—or so I thought. I was sixteen years old, a skinny, feral, lonely kid who had grown up longing for normal food, biting the heads off fleas, and never brushing my hair. Over the past years, a rage had grown up in me, the way rage might grow up in any animal that has its foot in a trap. It flew off of me, in sparks.

My emancipation in hand, I enrolled at Stadium High School in Tacoma. It was a castle-looking school of red brick, originally intended to be a luxury hotel but bankrupted and, after a couple of different lives, eventually made into a school. My old boyfriend Dean had moved away, so the "basement suite" at his mom's house was available. The deal was I'd pay thirty bucks a month to stay there. A new school, a kind mom upstairs: It seemed like I was set.

Chapter 12

I Was Just Getting Started as an Adult When...

The Community World Theatre, which sat on the corner of Fifty-Sixth and M Streets in Tacoma, was a small, black-box cement and brick theater that used to be something, then was a porno house, then became the music oasis I came to know and love. I saw so many incredible shows. So many seminal punk bands, so many forgotten ones, too. Fang, Flipper, Dag Nasty, Fugazi's first tour before they even had a record out. Bomb, Lush (Slim Moon from Kill Rock Stars' band), Malfunkshun, Dr. Know, Frightwig, Scream, Girl Trouble, SNFU, Beat Happening, Dangermouse, My Name—the list goes on and on. Music was the friend in the dark and the physical outlet that helped me shed some of the pent-up sorrow and frustration that roiled in my system. It was my family. It was when women played that I really took notice, like Portland's the Obituaries or the incredible band Tragic Mulatto, who were from San Francisco. Sadly, this did not happen near enough.

The thought that I might join a band or perform hadn't yet occurred to me. I was in this way still not far removed from the kid listening to AC/DC during a rained-out recess in elementary school—her toes moving, but not yet daring to do more. Music was reconfiguring my inner organs, but my vantage on it was as a fan, not as a possible musician. Something quavered in me, though, when Tragic Mulatto was playing—a lust I wasn't ready to heed. In the meantime, I used the Community World as a scrim to hide all of my many failings and threw all my energy into becoming a part of it, whether asked or not. I made posters for shows. I volunteered taking tickets or cleaning up. I was a lousy volunteer, but the owner, Jim May, didn't seem to mind too much. Jim was a tall, friendly, mop-haired ball of energy, then in his early thirties, who loved art and music and wanted our city to have a worthy punk scene. He, with the help of his wonderful network of friends made up of musicians, artists, writers, and oddballs, worked *hard* and joyfully and made incredible things happen. They were all older than me, but for some reason they let me hang around. No one tried to corrupt me, and maybe they even protected me a little. It was the healthiest thing I had going.

Community World aside, the only social life I had was based around heavy drinking. I drank, but not to the levels of the people I knew, since my mom had shown me how low it could take you. But among some of my friends it seemed like a race to see who could hit full-on messy alcoholic status. They tried to outdo each other, a competition to see who could get the most obliterated, as though destruction was harmless. It was the stupidest kind of rebellion. I was so lonely in that life, I slept with a few of the men in that scene. It was awful, but I just wanted someone's arms around me, and as cliché as that is, I managed to take it one step further to reach the nadir of cliché by just getting even *that* much lonelier. Thank god for my cassette tapes. I could at least disappear into music from time to time. I had the Bad Brains and the Meat Puppets. Mazzy Star and the Crucifucks. The Pogues and Nomeansno. The Cocteau Twins and the Cramps and obscure things taped off the radio late at night. They comforted me. They still do.

But then I didn't have enough money, even with the deal on rent. I had no money for food, and I'd be so famished at night I couldn't sleep or pay attention at school the next day. Dean's mom finally had enough. I'd let a kid I knew from the scene stay over on the couch and he'd repaid the good deed by racking up a sixty-eight-dollar phone bill calling *Greece* that I couldn't afford to pay back. Dean's mom looked heartbroken as she gave me the news I had to leave.

I couldn't argue. But it didn't solve the problem of where I would go.

There was only one person to call, and it was the person I least wanted to speak to. My mom. I dropped out of school and slunk back to her, and it was just as terrible as it had been before I left.

Begrudgingly, she said I could stay on the couch at her place. She had also been demoted from our old apartment in Gig Harbor to a one-bedroom trailer in Purdy, Washington, out on the peninsula. Back over the Narrows into the woods I went.

It was wintertime, and dark and dreary out there, and felt like so many steps backward. I missed the end of fall trimester as Christmas break came on. It was cold in the trailer and I tried to keep my head up by taking the bus into Tacoma once in a while. One day right before Christmas I took the bus to the mall to find my Gramma Mary Ann a present—she was still living two hours north, and Mom and I were going to see her at the holiday. I only had a tiny amount of money, but I found Gramma a nice burgundy scarf. I headed home on the bus satisfied that I had at least done *one* thing right. My mom was in bed when I got home, so I washed up, ate a couple of pieces of bread, and settled in on the couch to listen to music. In the morning I woke up a little happy. I loved my gramma and was excited to see her. I went to my mom's room to get her up, thinking she'd probably had too much to drink the night before. But her room was empty. Had she stayed with Chip, her unexceptional semi-boyfriend, the night before? When was she coming to get me in her little blue Subaru? An hour went by and still no Mom. Thank goodness we at least had a phone, so I called my grandmother collect. My mom was already there. She had just left me. No note, no nothing. It was fucking Christmas and she had just left me there in that cold trailer. My grandmother made her come get me.

It was a good, hard glimpse into what was to come.

Soon after, we ended up living with Chip, in his shit-brown, single-story "ranch"-style house in a subdivision called Burley, even farther out. There were lots of lazy white supremacists in that neck of the woods, just as there had been in Gig Harbor. It was a mean place, with unfriendly white people on all sides. It was impossibly remote, surrounded on two sides by water, and only accessed by two soggy, wet buses a day.

Wary of the drunk adults roaming the house, I built my bed in the closet of my little room by folding my foam mattress in half. At least I had my cat, Cammie. I'd have gone irreversibly dark without her. My mom and Chip were gone all the time, either at work or out drinking late. To avoid them when they were there, I would stay in my room with Cammie and listen to music. Music lived on my Pioneer turntable, my Marantz amp, and most importantly in my lavender off-brand, gas-station Walkman. I loved that thing to death.

When school came around again, I tried with all my heart to do good, but mostly I just listened to my imposter Walkman. Cranking Psi Com down the hallways of my shitty high school gave me a little rocket fuel to rise above the numbing, repetitive days. I could convince myself I was invisible.

But things at home were so awful, the cloud of it followed wherever I went. I hated Chip, who was a racist with some ill-informed hatred for the sovereign Indigenous tribes whose land the state of Washington existed on. He didn't think they had a right to anything. I thought otherwise, and I just couldn't keep my mouth shut. I truly hated him for so many reasons. He hated me, too, and I relished his dislike. The sweet, compliant kid I'd been in the past was long gone, and the beastly part of me spoiled for a fight, even at the risk of my own destruction. I had grown beyond reckless with my temper.

I had another guy music friend: Trevor Lanigan. He's the one who turned me on to Die Kreuzen, and we had a shared love of Nomeansno. We didn't hang after school or anything, but we had art class together and I had an unrequited crush on him. He had dark hair and brown eyes. He teased me a lot but wasn't an asshole. He went on to be in a band I loved, called My Name, with three friends who made me feel welcome in the world of music with them. Sometimes that year, on one of the many nights my mom and Chip were out getting hammered, Trevor would come all the way out just to smoke some weed or watch a movie. We'd laugh about dumb shit and talk about music. It was a serious kindness that really moved me.

Back then, I could tell who genuinely cared about me, but I still couldn't tell who "liked me." I didn't know what it meant if a guy was willing to come pick me up to hang out. I just figured they wanted to be friends, but on the other hand, why would they drive all this way if they didn't want to sleep with me? I mean, what could friendship with me possibly be worth? I had no answers then that weren't based in my sense of my own nothingness.

I didn't ever imagine love then. I could not.

One night, I woke to the sound of banging, which wasn't unusual since my mom and Chip came home loaded and clumsy most nights. But this time the din included Chip's voice cursing, yelling, with more than a whiff of danger in it. I got up and dragged myself down the short hall to the living room.

"What the hell?" I exclaimed in an agitated, unsure voice. "I have school tomorrow!"

"I'm sick of this shit!" he continued to rant. "I'm sick of you coming in late! Now you can just get out!"

He was talking to my mom, I supposed, but she wasn't there. He was throwing her stuff into boxes quite dramatically.

What do you expect from another drunk? I thought to myself. What an idiot. When I returned to my room, my heart was beating a little more shallowly, but where *was* my mom?

Not long after, I heard the door. I got up and again headed to the living room.

There she was, sitting sideways on the couch, looking half her already diminutive size, like an oily bird frozen on the beach. She was in shock.

"Your mom's been raped," said the ridiculous voice of Chip.

If you had asked me a day before, I would have told you I didn't care what my mom thought or did or what happened to her, and I would have meant it. She had grown so distant over the past years, I'd lost track of my affection for her entirely. But looking at her now, sitting on the blue flowered couch, the child in me rushed out. She had been so rare and precious through-out my life, the elusive sun in my sky. I knew then I loved her. Terribly. And she was hurt. My heart was in the car-crusher's jaws, exhaling breath and joy, and screaming in silence. This pain was pure terror. I was frozen, my eyes glazed open and tears squeezing out of the corners. I saw one hit the scab carpet like a water balloon where the hungry carpet drank it up. Now I was in shock, too.

I saw blood on her elbow.

"Mom, let's clean you up." I moved to help her from the couch. She stood robotically and started to walk. I noticed her prim jeans and her white fake Minnetonka moccasins she tried to un-scuff with cheap shoe polish, and her white socks. A rift of pity burst open in my gut in a deep ocean flume and flooded my senses, like when a diver rises too quickly to the surface; so dangerous, all the capillaries overfull and pulsing as if to rid themselves of blood completely. We somehow got to the bathroom, where I helped her take off her shirt and set it to the side. Her bra was a dirty white, pilled-up thing. Above her waistline two red eyes bored into me, two deep meaty wounds where she had bounced backward over the highway pavement when whoever it was had thrown her out the back of the van. I had no flashes or thought of my own rape. I was contorting myself completely into what she might need. I knew from experience she wouldn't want that part of me.

I wetted a washcloth and gently dabbed at one of her terrible cuts, my arms and hands not my own.

She winced and sucked her teeth when I touched her, as she did when concentrating on a small, intricate task, like threading a needle.

I pulled back. "We need to get you to the hospital," I said.

She didn't argue. I put the washcloth down on the edge of the sink. I saw the blood and lymph from my mom's body staining it. She found another shirt in her room and it was understood Chip would take her to the hospital. It was around 6:00 a.m. I had to go to school in an hour. I regret not going with her, but I, too, was in shock and could only do what came robotically. I don't remember walking to the end of that hateful cul-de-sac and waiting for the bus, but I know I must have.

The memory jags forward from there. It's now after school, and Mom is home from the hospital, on the same dark blue, flower-printed couch she'd been sitting on the night before. Someone knocked on the door and I opened it to a beige-and-forest-green police unit of a man, bulging a bit at the seams. As cliché would have it, he wore a dark mustache.

Once in the house he got right to it. She answered his glib, tossed-off questions politely, and after five minutes or so he was done. It became apparent that she knew the person who had raped her but wasn't going to tell the cop. I sat by, incredulous. Why wouldn't she tell him?! I couldn't understand it, despite the fact that I wouldn't tell anyone who *my* rapist was, either. But I had been a child. It had all flown over my head like a V of Canadian geese. I listened, confused and explosive and uncomprehending.

The cop got up to go. Rising, he said, "Well, it would be better if we got him on a drug charge anyway, 'cause then it might actually stick."

"You aren't going to try to find out who raped my mom?" I screamed. I charged toward him aggressively. He laughed nervously and said, "Nothing I can do about it if she won't give me a name," as he shut the door behind him.

The rape had plagued her with several health problems. She was in bed a lot and seemed more OK with my presence. I would make her BLTs. Chip remained as dumb as a saltine cracker and drunk as ever.

In private, I was confused, and now I understand something in me had been scraped open by what happened. I would badger my mom to tell the police who had hurt her. I wrote poetry about killing people. I alternated between listening to soft music, then aggressive music, to soothe myself. I began traveling to and from school with a steak knife in my pocket. I tried to do my work and take tests and seem normal.

I was so sad and angry that one day I had the bright idea of going to the school counselor for help. That's what they were for, right? As I sat in his office and recounted my story he stared blankly. Then he said, "I don't even know what to say to that."

Sitting across from him, my heart sank. What the fuck was the point of anything? The people who were supposed to help those of us in trouble were the most useless, compassionless drones who just wanted to be done with work. I flashed back to every teacher, every PSA advertisement, every church leader who ever said, "If you are in trouble, tell one of us."

A few days later I sat in my American history class while the basketball coach was giving us an oral quiz.

The teacher sped up a little too fast, and I raised my hand. "No, please, hold up! You're going too fast…"

He cocked his head and said, "I bet that's the first time you've ever said 'no' to anything."

I froze with shame. I'm so ashamed that I froze. I didn't finish my quiz. I wanted to cry but I didn't. I closed my book, the bell rang, and I made a pact with myself that I was done with high school forever.

A couple of days later I went back to get my things from my locker and was stopped by the kind Ms. Schneider, who taught English.

"What's going on? Why haven't you been in my class?" she asked.

I told her I was leaving, and I told her why.

She was horrified and I thought she was going to cry. I was

sorry I said anything, because I had just upset the only teacher in the whole place who was kind to me.

A friend had offered me a ride home to Chip's, but they couldn't take me till later, so I had to wait until the end of the day. I spent it in the art room with another friend, just decompressing over some music. When school was over, I headed to meet my friend with the car out front. I was almost out the double doors when, to my horror, I was being set upon by the basketball coach.

"Wait!" he was yelling. "Don't go, I'm sorry!"

Ms. Schneider must have given him HELL! Another reason never to tell *anyone* ANYTHING! "I understand why you are struggling, I was a hippie in the sixties..." His voice trailed off as I made a quick getaway, diving into my friend's car.

"DRIVE!"

Not long after this I heard he had to "leave" under suspicious circumstances.

There was a time, just a few years before, when I'd wanted to be an A student. The kind of teenager who does their homework and hopes to be tapped for the gifted program. Those days were done. I was dropping out of school. I had come face-to-face with the misogynist furnace that heated the whole system, and I wasn't going back.

My mom and Chip weren't happy I had dropped out, and lots of threats were made. I'd leave as soon as I woke up, even though it was dark in the mornings and often foggy. I'd found it a scary place even before my mom was assaulted; now it was a horror stroll, but staying home was actually scarier.

Every now and again my friend Drew would come pick me up and we'd go to the movies or a show or party. Most of the time, though, I was home, and most of the time it was a special kind of Pacific Northwest dark. A wet, impenetrable dark. I remember a few times a car pulling into the driveway and turning its brights on and just sitting there. It scared the shit out of me. Someone would call and hang up. I pleaded with my mom to come home from work, but she never did. Later, she told me that the man who raped her was someone she and Chip knew, and he would call and threaten her. He said he would kill her or me if she told anyone. This could easily have been a lie. My mom lied about a lot of things, though I didn't know it at the time. I was so depressed and scared I called my dad and Bill for help, but they had nothing to offer me.

Then it broke. It had to. All that week, the fight had been building. I had gone shopping at a thrift store and had gotten not just head lice, but also scabies from a knit hat I brought home. It took a few treatments of Kwell lotion and lice spray to get it under control. My mom insisted I keep it literally "under my hat" because Chip would be furious if he knew. It was exhausting and humiliating, since it had to be my filthy secret. I couldn't see my friends and I had come to the end of my rope. By some strange twist of fate, both my mom and Chip were home at dinnertime and we were all watching the news.

Chip made some bullshit comment about "those damn Indians" regarding fishing rights, and I lost it.

"You are such a fucking RACIST!" I yelled. I stood up.

Chip stood up, too, grabbed me by the throat, and attempted to pick me up. I clobbered him. I didn't care if I died. *Let him kill me* was all I felt coursing through my body. He let go, and I shrieked. If I was going down, he was coming with me.

My mom started screaming at me. He had tried to hurt me, and she had seen him do it. She wasn't even drunk and she had let him. My heart broke. I told my mom she was an evil cunt and asked how she could be OK with him hurting me like that? She didn't even try to defend herself. I had used the C-word and I was done. That was *way* worse than a grown man taking me in a choke hold. She told me to get out and not to come back.

I called my friend Mark, and he came and got me. I stayed with him and his sweet roommate in Bremerton for a couple of days and then limped home. I had nowhere else to go. I was back in my shitty room trying to get my mom to love me again. Once upon a time my mom had come back from the dead for me, but only to break my heart. It was one of the lowest places I have ever been. I tore apart everything in that room. Smashing glass, ripping books, destroying things I treasured from when I was little. I had looked into the eyes of those wounds on my mother's hip bones for her; it was the worst thing I'd ever seen, and I would have done it a million times more because *that's* how much I loved her. I would kill the man who did these things to her and live in jail forever. How did she not know? How had I failed so utterly?

I didn't know then that her silence should be respected—her rape wasn't mine to avenge. I lay with my face pressed to that fucking evil carpet. Shards of glass in everything: my clothes, my old schoolbooks not yet returned.

I have no idea how, but somehow I managed to get to Tacoma and look at an apartment with a friend. I borrowed money from my gramma for the down payment of $125. I got a job at the Stadium Thriftway as a chore monkey. I always had to clean the meat-cutting room, which was vile. My friend and I moved in together. If that hadn't happened when it did, I likely would have killed myself. I thought about it all the time.

That apartment was so nice, with new carpet, like someone actually cared that humans would be living there. We each had our own attic rooms with small, louvered windows that opened out. Mine was nestled into a huge horse chestnut tree. It was everything I wanted. I just needed to go get a few of my things and my cat.

I went to the corner pay phone at the Stadium deli to call my mom and let her know I'd be coming by to grab a load of my stuff the next day. I stood crunching on the hypodermic needles that littered the ground around the phone and dialed.

"Hello?" She was odd and stiff. "Um, I have some bad news…"

"Where's Cammie!?" I said.

My mom told me that Cammie, my beloved cat, had died in the night.

"WHAT THE FUCK HAPPENED!?" I cried, desperate, as if I could somehow reverse it.

Cammie had been attacked by a neighbor's dog early in the day. They hadn't even tried to get her to a vet. She had bled out on that blue flowered couch. My sweet friend had suffered, and my mom just let it happen. I gasped for air, I was crying so hard. I was angry and grief stricken and just sick. I hung up the phone. I didn't care who saw me; I gripped the sides of the pay phone shroud and hung on, sobbing into my arm.

I already knew this about my mom, but this incident underscored it: Things left in her care died. She would not protect them. She would not try to save them. Even as I grieved for Cammie, some part of me registered how lucky I was to have gotten out from under that roof.

There are so many dumb clichés out there about rape. A few seem like they might be meant to help you process it but are actually ways to gloss over the messiness of what happened. They use words like "resilience" and "character." One of the bad ideas is that forgiveness is the ultimate act of courage. It's not. I don't believe forgiveness is something you can actively *do* with any realness or sincerity. It's not a tangible "act," in the same way that justice is not an act. Maybe forgiveness and justice are somehow the same state of being.

Maybe forgiveness comes later, and maybe it never does. Maybe you are so evolved you can feel it right in the moment of betrayal. I have forgiven people and events before, and it's usually after a long time and self-searching about something completely *different*. Forgiveness seems to be a sweet, brief rest at the crossroads of *other* things. It's almost a divine by-product. It's not a tiny golden diploma you bestow upon someone. Forgiveness takes many forms and may be as simple as the moment something no longer has power over you.

That doesn't mean that there aren't good ideas about forgiveness and its beauty, but if something doesn't stir anything but contempt in you, there's a reason. Trust your contempt. Dissect it if you can. The reason your contempt is tapping you on the shoulder may be in there, and be valid, or it may not. If you can't find it, it's OK. That doesn't mean you should canonize your rage, either, just make sure you take it seriously. If you learn nothing from something horrible, you are human, and that doesn't make you soulless or cruel. Sometimes bad things are just senseless brutality that finds you. You do not deserve or ask for these things. They are not always teaching you a lesson.

Chapter 13

Meet the Del Logs

I walked everywhere in Tacoma, getting to know its neighborhoods and their spidery satellites by heart. I fantasized about living in the north end in a real house of my own. The apartment buildings and massive houses there were the future to me. I couldn't live in any of those beautiful places since I was too poor, but I could walk the streets at night and gaze in the windows and dream about it. I liked to go barefoot in the summer and walk through the alleys. The pavement was made with tiny, rounded pebbles and often had patches of moss, so it was easy on the feet, unless you encountered a spiny horse chestnut pod. Some alleys were still made from the old smooth ballast bricks that came from England on ships that would dump them and return with timber. I would wear pajama bottoms and a T-shirt, sliding along as silently as possible, occasionally encountering a friendly feline or two.

Walking at night soothed me, like there was less consciousness to contend with. I wasn't so on edge and my cyclonic churning could ebb a little. When I was outside, and in motion, I was pleasantly peaceful, despite the fact that what I was doing was terribly dangerous. Even after what I'd just seen happen to my mom, and what I'd gone through myself at fourteen, I couldn't keep from the necessary wandering; it provided a simultaneous thrill and deep calm. I was too wild and without outlet, so tired from surviving in the world that I wasn't going to be kept indoors on principle. I could not be contained. Often if I was out in nature or at a park, I'd have an anxious feeling—like there was always something I was *supposed* to be doing or that I was going to regret *not* doing if I dared relax. But that feeling was never with me on those nocturnal walks through the city. Some nights I'd sit on the swings at the Annie Wright School and listen to songs on my faux Walkman. It was as close to the home I wanted as I could get.

I wasn't driving yet, and I didn't really know how. I had tried to drive friends' cars, with their supervision, of course, a couple of times but not with any regularity. Just enough to know the basic concepts. But I had realized long ago that even the barest freedom in the world I lived in would mean having a car. When I was with my friends who had cars we felt an elation in the movement and listening to the tape deck and going somewhere *we* wanted. I knew the only way to feel that freedom on my own was to buy one and get it over with. I had no rich relatives who were gonna buy me one for my "sweet sixteen," which was two years gone anyway. I'd have to do it myself. I saved some money and borrowed some and bought a 1964 Ford Falcon for $350.

I had spotted the car in a classified ad in the back of the Tacoma *News Tribune*. It didn't quite work, but then the ad hadn't claimed that it did. It was one of the only cars in my price range, but also I was very excited that it was the same model the Rodriguez brothers drove in the movie *Repo Man*. It was a faded yellow, which I referred to as "buckskin." Looking the car over, I was reminded of my dad out in our front yard, with his truck engines in various states of "running." A few friends helped me fix up the Falcon enough so it could limp along. But now that I had the car, I had no one to teach me how to drive it. I could have asked someone, but I hesitated. In my mind I'd already asked too much.

I was six stories off the ground in the Walker Apartments. I had lived a few places since my roommate left our first apartment. I faced eastward, toward the impossibly huge Mount Tahoma and the trickster moon, which bounced its silver beams off the top of the glacial cap of the mountain and into the window of my little studio, like a stone skipped into the apartment. I dreamt so hard there. My new car rested loyally between the orange slanted parking lot lines below, looking like a gateway in the moonlight; my horse, my dragon, some longer legs, an Amazon bow...ready to become an extension of me. I would sometimes go down and clean it lovingly, admiring its beautiful rectangular Aztec angles and Spartan design. I didn't care that the seats were rusting through the floor of its unibody frame in brown, scabby flakes, I loved it wholly.

One night I couldn't take it anymore. It was around 9:00 p.m., quiet and warm and clear. I decided I *had* to drive. Insurance had just been made mandatory and of course I had none (who could afford that?). But consequences be damned, I couldn't wait forever. I snuck down the six flights of stairs and padded barefoot across the still-warm street to my new friend, in the same way I liked to slink around the neighborhood in the dead of night. There was danger, yes, but also exhilaration. I understood the stakes were high: a ticket? arrest? my life? someone else's life? But I knew I was going to do this. I just couldn't make *any* mistakes. It was that simple.

I got into the Falcon and clicked my wide lap belt, and the engine turned over faithfully the first time. I very carefully backed out of the parking spot, checking and rechecking for cars or any other obstacle. Once in the lane, I put it in drive and began. I was so excited and agitated. It didn't matter where I went, I basked in the silver of the streetlights and the breeze of summer air that *I* was pulling in through the open windows. I was powerful and tiny and hyperalert. I didn't stop anywhere, just drove in widening Etch-a-Sketch rectangles through the neighborhood. I would never go backward; I would drive forever. I would become good at it, taking stupid risks but always respecting the car's power, and the power it gave *me* as the little Amazon I was. Something had clicked up to full height, something was complete. When I returned to my apartment, I was quite high.

I describe this first ride in such detail as there was a potency to it, a feeling of something slotting into place, and that was also happening during this time with music making.

Not far into my new life in Tacoma, I'd gone over to the

house of my friend Bill Henderson, from the band Girl Trouble. Bill, Kurt Kendall, and I were hanging out in his basement (complete with life-sized model of "Chairy" from *Pee-wee's Playhouse*), and Bill popped in a copy of a copy of a videotape of music clips he'd gotten from his sister and bandmate, Bon. It was some cool movie scenes, some videos, clips of cartoons, and other odd things. A song or two went by and then suddenly I was caught in the tractor beam that was the Flat Duo Jets. It was a snippet from the movie *Athens, GA: Inside/Out* and they were performing the song "Crazy Hazy Kisses." A two-person band originally out of North Carolina, they consisted of Dexter Romweber on guitar and Chris "Crow" Smith on drums. They were pure nitroglycerine. I wanted to *be* their music; I felt like I already half was. They tapped into some feral vein that ran to the center of the earth, like a stick of dynamite that could control how much it exploded while still preserving its sweating cylinder. They were, in a word, impossible. Something unlocked for me that day—still inchoate, still not yet fully formed, but a way that making music could become a physical manifestation of the blazing wild horse energy inside my body, of how I might have all my old gods and new gods together. This was a new kind of love that hit me like a lightning bolt from the sky. Not a romantic love, but an all-consuming one.

Soon after, my friend Greg Lenti mentioned that he wanted to start another band. He had a great little apartment attached to his dad's place out in Fife to rehearse in. I said I wanted to play drums. I had been playing on a snare with a practice pad on top, and I liked the feeling of it, of raising my arms up and then bringing them down with my whole body. Playing on my own, I'd thought I didn't sound so bad. I could keep time, at least at *one* speed! I'd become addicted to the feeling and the movement of drumming. It was so forceful and certain, like hammering iron. There was a satisfaction to it, too, like how I used to feel as a kid twirling my fake baton and enjoying how strong my arm looked. And because I was shy, being partially hidden behind a large drum set in the back was appealing—I could be there but not there, part of the unit, but also separate.

Laura Woods joined on vocals and Andy Reetz on bass. Greg played guitar. We called ourselves the "Del Logs." There were a couple bands with "Del" in their names rattling around in the eighties, the Del-Lords and the Del Fuegos, and their music was so fast and slick that for some reason we thought it would be funny to slow the whole "Del" thing down by throwing a log around its neck. We had grown up in a cold and rainy place, so we likened ourselves to the kind of fake fireplace logs that glow electric neon-orange in the gloom. All the layers of "meaning" made us laugh: the Del Logs. We would buy half racks of Old Milwaukee or whatever was on sale and hang out at Greg's little house, which was basically a living room with a bath and a kitchenette, and bang away. It was truly joyous. I loved getting lost in the patterns and the crescendos and the stops and starts. It was appealing to my Virgo nature to "organize" in this way. Our number-one fan was a filthy gray turkey who lived next door that we named Frank. She would walk right through the open sliding glass door in summer and gobble enthusiastically at the bass drum. From my drum stool I could see her beady little eyes taking in the drum set, drawn in by the shiny parts. She would pick up her scaly little dinosaur feet very slowly and walk back and forth in front of me, her filthy pewter feathers spattered in mud. She left giant poops everywhere.

All in all, the Del Logs only ever played two shows, one at a house party at Laura's and the second at the famous Bob's Java Jive in Tacoma. I got to make the poster, which choked me up, like I'd come full circle. I was making a poster for a show *I* was going to play in. With meticulous attention, I steered my hand around the page, drawing out the words "THE DEL LOGS" and the date. A jittery elation vibrated through my body—I knew without a doubt this was the highlight of my life so far.

All through childhood I'd felt some call of a wild energy. If I'd been feral before, now that feralness had at last found a purpose. It was in place to protect me. It was my "shield-up" position. What does "feral" look like on a musician? I think of this example: One night I am playing and singing so hard, with such concentration, and suddenly I feel a gnat fly into my eye. I can't do anything about it, so I continue. After the show, I examine my eye and see glimpses of the black gnat as I roll my eyeball to one side and the other. But no matter how I try, I can't extract it, so I resign myself to the fact that it is now beyond me, and that I will just digest the gnat, as though my eye has morphed into a Venus flytrap or some other carnivorous plant. It was now its own separate creature, digesting an insect on its own time. And I, the bigger beast, the ultimate host, was digesting all the other creatures within it. I had to be careful and check around internally to make sure that I wasn't digesting my *own* organs. I was that voracious, that ravenous.

At this time, I was mostly making drawings and flyers for

shows, but I also collaged and made costumes and little sculptures. I loved the surrealists and Edward Hopper. I liked the mystery they didn't feel obligated to solve. I took a lot of art history classes at the community college, which left me hungry, since so few women artists were represented. Most of what we saw, man after man after man, gave me no nutrients. It's as if the information actually *fed* on me, leaving me depleted.

Music and driving will always be intertwined for me, and how I came to music—sidling toward it from a sideways position—was the same way I took to driving. After I got the Ford Falcon, I wouldn't get a license for two more years and drove illegally all that time. I didn't have the money for a driving test and license; and school and my jobs ate up all my time. It wasn't for lack of wanting to be legit; legality just eluded me.

The funny thing was I could still *buy* and own cars. After selling the Falcon to a friend, I ended up buying a 1963 AMC Rambler Classic 660, and I paid all of fifty bucks for it. It had a battery-eating problem that turned out to just be a faulty ground wire. It was a tank with a bronze coat of paint and four doors, which made it horribly uncool to gearheads, since only two-doors were considered cool. "How dare someone snub you because you are efficient!" I'd say as I stroked my hand along the bulletproof submarine flank of the dash. How I loved that car! The engine compartment was so large I could stand *inside* the gap between the body of the car and the engine. It was a straight six, which meant the oil filter and spark plugs, air filter and carburetor were on top and very accessible. This made me that much keener to work on it myself. I took pride in it the same way that I took pride in playing drums in a band. I wanted to see what my brain could do in these realms that had been ever so softly, but still unmistakably, cordoned off as forbidden to my "female" hands. I wanted to unknot my chromosomes and rebraid them into something else; something not wholly "male" but not "female," either. I was pushing toward a blurry result I could not yet comprehend, but I pushed as though there was a raging forest fire at my back and Bambi, the rest of the woodland creatures, and I needed to get the fuck out. My consciousness was urgent and sometimes angry. I would play drums with ferocity and fix my own car with capability and who knows what else?

On warm weekends I'd put on my cutoff coveralls, go to the auto parts store, pick up some small thing, and head home to work on the Rambler. I have never really liked beer except on a hot day while working on my own car, so I'd set one on the roof and lose myself in a task. Something about beer was the perfect complement to the smells of gas and grease. I was good at gapping spark plugs (I kept a gapper on my key chain, and not just for show like some rockabilly dickhead) and adjusting the idle and diagnosing any problems my sweetheart might have. I kept that old Rambler running at peak as long as I owned it. I didn't want to be beholden to other people, especially strangers, to fix the car for me, and not just because I couldn't afford it. Its radio glowed aqua blue-green, and I listened to the oldies station or just traveled with a Walkman to listen to tapes illegally as I drove along. I had a little confidence for once. I was moving, the car was working, because of me, because of what I could do.

I had long since moved on from the Thriftway by then and was now working at a crappy chain day care and taking more community college classes at night. I had no money. Since everyone I knew was poor, we were all a little angry, so I didn't really think I was unusual in that regard. Plus, we found lots of joy in our little city; we even made it from scratch.

My anger was also tied to some weird ambition and survival mode, all three very separate in a healthy person, not so much for a young person who was also a bit of a twitchy tidal wave. My rage turned and turned and gained momentum as it never hit anything, resolved anything, or made anything better. It was just an iffy weather system. But it did create energy. Some bad, some good; the bad part drilled me into the ground, filled my mouth and nostrils with dirt and smothered me with despair. The good was OK, like the part that loved to be part of a crowd, lost in the pulse of live music. I wanted strangers to know not to fuck with me, like a fluorescent sea cucumber or a striped yellow jacket. I was stingy *and* poisonous! I was willing to fight anyone. It was *dumb*, but what other choice did I have? There was no parent's house to go to if I needed to hide from someone. I knew and respected many women like this. I knew the consequences of being "nice." Fuck that. At times I was a bubbly diplomat who wanted to think the best of people, but also a harsh badger if you messed with me or my friends. I didn't forgive easily and I could hold a grudge like it was my pensioned government job.

My friends and I gathered music from every possible source. Indie and used record stores, thrift shops, yard sales, taping off the radio and TV, buying stuff at shows, mixtapes. The cheaper the better. We were all so hungry for anything weird or new, anything that looked through a portal to a place where things were *happening* and changing. The music made me imagine the desert Southwest, or sunny California and Australia, or gray, serious England. I wanted to go to every place music whispered to me about.

We shared music with each other like we all needed it to survive, which I believe we did. We lived in unfinished basement apartments and rock and roll houses and apartment buildings, warehouse rooms, old theaters, and even the former Nihongo Gakko Japanese language school on Tacoma Ave. Often without proper heat. Northwest cold is hard to avoid no matter how many layers you are wearing. I spent many nights trying to do homework in front of an open hot oven. We had to focus on something else. So we had music.

Even though I would have killed to be in a band on tour, I didn't dare envision that for myself. The womanless darkness of the punk scene was spawning things like riot grrrls in Olympia, but my town was still too poor and scattered. For a time, there had been the Fifty-Sixth Street House and Community World, but then Community World closed, and nothing sprang up to take its place. We relied on house parties and a couple of gay bars, like the Loop and the Polar Bear. The Polar Bear was *beautiful*, from the neon sign out front to the dance music. It was heavenly and safe, and the people I met there opened other doorways. The suspense of what the world could be was killing me. I wanted to meet *everyone*.

But still, there was something holding me back. At nineteen, I had started seeing a guy who was a tour manager for some famous bands in Seattle. We were at some show and there were lots of well-known people from a bunch of different bands hanging out. At some point in the evening, Jennifer Finch from L7 ran up to my boyfriend and gave him a warm hug. He greeted her with joy. They took no notice of me, and he didn't introduce us. I was *really* pissed, but not because he didn't introduce me or because he was hugging another woman. I was pissed because *I* wasn't *ready* to meet her, and in that moment, I had *made* myself invisible to them both. It was a psychotic subconscious reaction to her. She was "complete." I was just a liquid nobody, dying to be fully formed, important, useful, interesting, funny. But I wasn't in a band anyone knew, and as far as I could tell I wasn't funny, or interesting, or any of those things. I was in transition to my adult self, and deep down I believed I'd never have anything she would be interested in.

What a shitty thing to put on a stranger. I was just so desperate *not* to be seen as someone's eager little idiot girlfriend. It's like I was saying to her, "You can't see me like this! I'm not done yet!" And instead of having the insight to realize it, I just felt ashamed and took it out on L7. I told my boyfriend I thought they "sucked." He took offense, since they were friends of his, but I didn't care. I just kept shooting myself in the foot till I emptied the gun. That is what jealousy looked like on me, and I was so jealous she could walk right up to people and hug them with no hesitation, loud and joyful. I was jealous that her makeup was smeared a bit and she didn't give a fuck. She *knew* who she was and fully inhabited herself in a way that should have inspired me (it does now), but I hated myself so much that being close to her confidence just turned me sour.

On the one hand I wanted to stretch and run and amaze everybody—and on the other I wanted to melt into the wall.

While I was still living in Tacoma, I went down to the auto parts store to pick up a carburetor gasket for the Rambler. I met a mechanic named Blue. A tall guy, rangy and red-headed, he reminded me a little of my dad, who was still off in Alaska. Perhaps it was his beard. We struck up a conversation about old American cars while waiting for the employees to find our desired parts in the back. I could tell I neither annoyed nor challenged him, which put me at ease. I told him I was looking for help fixing something that was out of my league. He said he could do it after garage hours or on the weekend at his place, since I didn't have much money. It was better for him to get paid under the table anyway.

The next weekend I drove across town to where he lived with his sister in the south end, off Pac Avenue. It was a run-down, white, two-story house that had seen better days. His sister was a larger woman with an oxygen tank who wasn't hostile or friendly, just completely uninterested in us. We went out back to his trampled-flat, crabgrassy yard, which smelled of used motor oil and cigarettes, and set to work troubleshooting possible problems with the Rambler's generator. Well, Blue did, and I assisted. After we finished and my car was healthy again, I paid him in cash and thanked him heartily. We both cracked a beer and lit up a cigarette; a tradition after a day of weekend car work.

We talked about cars we loved; I was into smaller sixties sedans and Blue liked pretty much anything with a big engine.

He drove a 1978 burgundy Monte Carlo. He had a few cars in the backyard in various states of disassembly. He pointed to a large white Buick, which looked like an injured predator.

"Wanna try your hand at rebuilding a carburetor? That Special needs some attention." The engine was a 325-horsepower, 401-cubic-inch Wildcat V-8. A true muscle car.

I did want to try, and so the next Saturday I found myself removing and disassembling a huge four-barrel carb. I was in my element. Blue worked away on his own project but came over every so often to give advice or instruction. Since the carburetor had to soak in gas to get the gunk off, I'd need to keep coming back to Blue's house until it was finished. I was so excited I told my friends and bandmates what I was up to. They were all skeptical that some random mechanic in his thirties would want to help me fix cars and figured there was lust afoot on Blue's behalf, but I didn't think so. There was something lonely about Blue, extremely solitary, that I identified with. He felt familiar to me.

I went back and finished that carburetor. I bought the parts and did the work. Under Blue's guidance, I put it back on the Special's engine and started it up with great anticipation and excitement. It roared to life, a black cloud of dust and smoke shooting out the back. I was overjoyed and could see Blue's happiness, too. He even seemed a little proud. When we finished, he told me the car was mine if I wanted it and signed the title over. I was beyond grateful, and even a little proud of myself. It was an enormous act of kindness, that gift. It would take years before I realized that it wasn't just Blue's beard that reminded me of my dad. It was his solitariness, too, the way he held himself separate from the world.

Working together had been some sort of dream version of how my dad and I could have been together, not a traditional father-daughter, but two peers working away together in a yard full of broken, beat-up cars, trying to get them back into running shape.

Chapter 14

Eyes Swiveled Forward

I was twenty-two years old when I met Chauncey. It's odd—I think there are ways we all want our stories to be different, big or little details we would change if we could. If I had my way, I would have found my way to everything that happened next just by following my nose and intuition. But that's not what happened.

I'd gone with friends to the Crocodile Cafe in Seattle to see a band he was in. I liked this band—they played energetic danceable garage rock. We had a lot of mutual friends and were introduced after the show. He was a tall, pink eraser of a man, dark haired, awkward, and funny. We hit it off, but I didn't think too much about it. I was coming off a bad dating streak that had left me with all the romantic yearning of a frozen piece of rock cod. It was nice to meet someone and not automatically think about them as romance material, to just be glad to have a new pal.

Later, I went along with some friends who were playing a show alongside Chauncey's band in Vancouver, Canada. We piled into a long white van, driving over the Lions Gate Bridge on a rare gorgeous January night. Everything was blanketed with snow, and the van moved in and out of the pools made by streetlights. Everything sparkled. Enchanted.

We'd been invited to have dinner at Chauncey's parents' house first, where he still lived. It was a sweet little house, lit up against the snowy, tidy lawn. Inside, it was packed—his parents, his big sister, tons of friends, too. Everyone was so jolly, and there was a big pot of veggie pea soup on the stove and lots of crusty bread to dip into it. I sat on the couch with the soup balanced on my lap. A Currier and Ives print of Niagara Falls hung over the fireplace, the falls like an Ice Age basin of frosty blue water, with a little island in the middle populated by prehistoric-looking trees and a family picnicking. My gaze kept going to his parents. His dad and mum were British. They were both so nice, just laughing and welcoming everyone who came in. It was so crazy to see a middle-class family who got along, parents who liked their kids, *and* their kids' *friends*? And then they were gonna come to the show?

As I was eating, I avoided looking at Chauncey, just noticing out of the corner of my eye that he was wearing flooded flares. He seemed bizarre to me, and I felt a little embarrassed, experiencing a little thrum of revulsion whenever I saw the hem of those pants. It is, I know now, exactly how I've felt every time I've ever fallen in love.

We pressed on from the house to the show, which was held at a community center across the street, a plunge into a loud and sweaty bath, then the group of us from Washington packed back into the van and drove the three hours home. I sat in the back, letting the conversation wash over me, the tape deck playing some mixtape. We were like a pack of dogs who've had a great day—tired, lighthearted, piled up together.

A little while later, Chauncey's band was playing a show in Tacoma and I invited them to crash at my house. By the end of that weekend, Chauncey and I were together. It seemed to happen in fast-forward; one minute we hardly knew each other at all and the next we were completely entwined. He loved music the way I did, and I liked how funny he was. There was a sweetness to him, too, a quality that I now know had to do with growing up beloved and sheltered, but at the time I just experienced him as a wondrous, otherworldly companion, less jagged and feral than I was but somehow still compatible. During the first year we were together we'd go get Slurpees and sit in the car listening to music and talking, and the sweetness of those drinks—so icy and soothing, one of the only bright spots from my childhood when it wasn't slapped out of my hand by a bully as I walked home—is all laced through that year. It was like the high school romance I'd never had, and it felt amazing to be loved and to have found someone to love, after so long. Someone who wanted to build their life around music, too.

It felt so good in fact that I moved mountains—or at least myself, my cat, Betty, and all my stuff—to Vancouver for college.

I had gotten into the Emily Carr College of Art and Design in Vancouver. My dad was pleased; my mom kept her silence. She had long ceased caring what happened to me.

Chauncey was still living with his parents to "save money," so I moved into the second floor of a Vancouver special, a two-apartment unit of a type only produced en masse in British Columbia. Mine was on East Eighth Avenue. My roommate was a guy named Kev, who'd play me records as I sat on the floor working on my projects for school. The carpet was pink and smelled like flea spray. My first year we leaned heavily into Mott the Hoople, and I'd sing along with "Alice" as I cut pop cans with tin snips, using the metal to trim out some art project or another. After Kev went to bed, I'd stay up and watch reruns of *Northern Exposure* and do the journaling work required for class.

I had started finding other people to play music with, too, and my weekly schedule was hectic. I had school all day. Homework. I had my car, but, as in Tacoma, I liked to walk everywhere, except for the two nights a week I took the Sky-Train to band practice. Getting from place to place on foot took up an amazing amount of time, but I listened to so much music while I walked, and the exercise was good for me. I was always carrying way too much, though: drum parts, water, art supplies, all packed away into a backpack. Inside that bag might be anything from a large, awkward portfolio to a discarded metal object and enough books to anchor a crane.

Always on the edge of being late, I walked fast through any weather.

The sky was neon gray most of the time, with low-ceiling, uniform clouds stretched across it. A lot of people are tipped into seasonal depression by this, but I liked it—the close, gray sky made the world feel like a cozy room, and it set expectations low when you stepped outside. Like "Do not worry you're going to miss out on some grand natural event, it's not happening." Instead, it was a lot of tiny needle rain, drizzle, and light fog. Every surface was wet. Once in a while, it would get cold enough to softly ice over. There would be tiny frost patterns on the aluminum-sill windows and across the sidewalks.

I was an odd-looking creature at the time, like a little half-turned werewolf. Back claws poking out, tail tucked into the back of my pants, which were often just a pair of blue men's long johns with a Y-front wiener-hatch in the front and ripped knees. I would pair these "pants" with a black fake-fur coat I'd gotten out of the free box in the basement laundry room of my building. I thought I was THE shit in my long johns and fur coat. I'm not sure what it was about men's long johns that I loved so much, but I think it was about comfort and not really identifying so much as a girl.

One day at a practice, my new bandmate, CC, took umbrage with a particularly bad outfit—a pair of cut-off, railroad-striped overalls with men's white long johns (also with ripped knees) underneath.

"What are you *wearing*?!" she gaped.

We both stood still for a moment, taking in my outfit.

I was an old prospector?

"No!?" she said, shaking her head in disbelief, like a big sister scolding me on a bad decision for my own good. We laughed *really* hard.

CC and her friend Tobey had drafted me to play drums in a band called Meow, which we later had to change to "Maow" due to another band already having the name. I was not given a choice about joining. Tobey and CC just announced it was happening, which we all found as hilarious as the prospector underwear I'd wear to our practices. They didn't have to insist too hard, anyway—I was game. Tobey and CC became two of my best rock and roll feminist teachers and friends. We were all young and imperfect, ferocious and high energy. We were crude and silly and in love with adventure, possibility, and, most important, music.

CC was freckled and had strawberry-blond hair. I'd say she was on the diminutive side, but she was so strong and forceful I never thought of her that way. She was an incredible artist and was trying to get into the film industry as a set decorator. I've never known another person with such a gift for using color. She was our bass player.

Tobey was tall but slight, with doe eyes, dark hair, a great laugh, and a boyish way about her. She considered herself uptight, which I never really found her to be. She was just careful and had an opinion. She was honest and spoke her mind, even if what she had to say might not be terribly popular, which

I valued and respected her for. She played guitar. We were a trio and we loved each other. (We *still* love each other.)

We wrote most of our songs together, and we all sang, joyful and cacophonous. We clanged and pitched our voices out like fishing nets. We didn't go about it in any formulaic way, just having fun. During our years of playing together, we underwent many trials and tribulations, made our way through many confrontations and arguments, but mostly we had a blast.

One reckoning came when Maow was entered in an epic-style, multiweek battle of the bands, put on by the nearby university's indie radio station, CITR. Our band was the only one composed solely of women, and we didn't take ourselves super seriously. We wore homemade fur bikinis that looked more like huge diapers than anything sexy—they lampooned the idea of "sexiness," just like our songs did. We practiced as hard as anyone else and put so much heart into what we were doing, we just never lost sight of the fun.

Weeks went by, and we were still in the game. Strangely, every time we won, I felt embarrassed. It was a creeping discomfort that made me brush off our achievement when speaking to other people.

That final night after we played, I said to someone, "We suck. We won't win anyway."

CC had had enough by then, and she read me the riot act.

"Do *not* say that shit anymore!" she implored. "We work just as hard if not harder than anyone else! We *practice* and care about what we are doing! Sure, it's for *fun*, but what you're saying is fucked up and takes away from what we are doing!"

Slowly, I took in that she wasn't just mad—she was hurt.

She was, of course, 100 percent correct. Deep inside, my ambition felt forbidden, and the feeling of "winning" made my covetous self want to slither away and hide, like desire and ambition were something obscene. *That* was the feeling that made me reflexively say "we suck" after every win—like I had no place in me to hold success, just this weird little crevice inside where I'd hide away what I wanted. I was so grateful CC was the first person to challenge me and make me notice what felt so automatic: the bit of magic I would do without even thinking, Here's something good, I'll turn it into something bad. I wasn't just hurting myself with it, I was hurting my bandmates.

In the end, Maow won, beating two bands made up of dudes in the final round. One of the bands was very gracious and seemed to understand good sportsmanship and also that this wasn't a Nobel Prize. They had done it for fun, just as we had, and we all became immediate friends. The other band thought they had the contest in the bag and weren't happy when they lost. They said some shitty things about our abilities to the station's paper in their drunken, sour-grapes haze. Interestingly, the paper didn't reach out to interview us, and we had won *their* contest.

We were baffled. The sexism was so...obvious. We had a good friend who wrote for the paper who I basically bullied (it's a fine line when you are an American trying to convince a polite Canadian to do something, even if bullying is not your intention) into writing an article about Maow. I wrote the questions and all the answers, and it was printed. But we felt no satisfaction, just that justice had been served. The necessary machinations it took to see our band in print sucked all the joy out of it.

I was figuring out the teeter-totter that anyone who makes things and puts them out in public eventually grapples with. What's the right way to talk about yourself? What's a healthy amount of self-promotion? What's too much? It can be tricky for almost anyone to figure out, but I was especially wobbly.

There were still so many connections I hadn't made in my understanding of the world, awkward in some ways yet firmly present in others. I was so saturated by male violence by the time I was twenty-two, fighting to come out of my shell since being raped at fourteen and witnessing the aftermath of my mother's rape when I was eighteen. All of it made me volatile, bold, self-deprecating, shy, angry. Raw. I wasn't going to let myself or other women down anymore. I would protect them, whether physically *or* with my loud mouth—I was sincere but not always sure how to execute it.

I look back and all I see is that wounded critter being swept up in a seismic growth spurt so late in coming. I was trying to breathe underwater and dog-paddling as fast as I could. I have a hard time remembering my own kindnesses and loyalty during this period, even though I know they were present. I was just so aggressive. Thank god for drums.

Being in the insulated environment of college sheltered me from thinking about what I wanted. I had no idea how to even *begin* to ask that question. My life seemed to be on the upswing; how could I *dare* to ask for or want anything more? That was for men like my boyfriend, Chauncey. Everything came *to* him; he didn't have to go out and get it. In front of me was an amorphous, foggy vision of some kind of future in graphic art. Music was my obsession, but there was no way I would admit to myself it's what I really wanted. I'd been beaten over the head by the

Reagan-era idea that arts and music were "pipe dreams" that were just barely acceptable as "hobbies," let alone as life goals. And I was a girl, making it all that much worse. Even though I wasn't, not really.

I listened to music like it was more important than eating and breathing. I went nowhere without my portable cassette player and shitty headphones. If the batteries went out or I forgot a specific tape, it could easily ruin my day. At home I listened to my own record collection as well as my roommate's, who worked in a record store. I watched Canadian music television and sang in the shower. There must always be music so I wasn't alone with myself. But I didn't know that at the time, I just thought I was a fan. That was at least 75 percent of it. The other 25 percent was dangerous and therefore went unexamined.

I'd meet other people on occasion who were musicians and artists. Some were hurling themselves forward like they were trying to bust through a chain-link fence. Others merely eddied frantically, spinning their wheels, not realizing they weren't moving ahead. Some were too fast and believed in the idiotic "sex, drugs, and rock and roll" to an embarrassing degree. Others were kneecapped by their own competitive energy, which has no place in creative music making. Some were supernovas of inspiration and generosity.

I wasn't naturally an alpha personality, but I eventually became one out of sheer disbelief and mild disgust. "Are we here to practice or not? Put the bong down!" (Not Maow, though. They always had their minds on practice.) I played with plenty of people who I thought took their talent for granted. Really, they just had different reasons for playing. They were OK with the fun, relaxing, social parts of making music in Vancouver. I wanted to talk to every person on earth, which meant practicing and getting the fuck on the road. I wanted to meet *everyone*. I wanted to play for all the people *everywhere*!

Maow worked *hard* and we loved it. We had eyes positioned in the front of our skulls, like the predator mammals we were. We only saw forward. We were *hungry* for landscape and experience. We burned it all up with our eyes and our bodies, like little forest fires. We were pure appetite.

Chapter 15

High, Higher

I began singing with Maow, and during my first years in Vancouver I never sang alone. I always felt my voice sounded nasally: oversized and mulish. It doesn't fold into harmonies easily (not that I knew what harmonies even *were!*), not even with itself; it's a blunted point of a shape with no vibrato. *All the great singers have vibrato!* I wanted to sing like Bessie Griffin, who had a vibrato like a strobing wave machine. While I'm quite loud, we all know that doesn't mean much. I'm not ungrateful for my voice, and I've worked very hard over the years to become a better singer; I just never felt like I fit anywhere, simple as that. My voice is neither pretty nor powerful, and despite the fact that I can breathe like a motherfucker and hold a looooooooong note, it may not be the note I want to sing. I always dreamed of possessing a caramelly low end to my register, a velvety charcoal scrape, but I have higher frequencies that are closer to a dentist's drill than a foghorn. I'm not willing to smoke my way to huskiness, so I have to make do. Don't get me wrong, I wouldn't trade my own voice for anyone else's, but I did feel quite awkward and naked a lot of the time starting out, especially when I sang with other people.

Singing along with Tobey and CC in Maow gave me some confidence. One day I was writing a line for the band and I asked which one of them wanted to sing it. CC said, "YOU sing it!" It was that simple.

I'd long worshiped the Cramps, gospel music, and my gramma's country music, and something about that and my interests in art, books, and folktales made me want to swerve hard toward singing songs with stories behind them. I decided I wanted to be a country singer, which admittedly was a bit of an odd choice. I couldn't even really explain it. But I had been listening to country my whole life and I realized many of its women were way more punk than anything going on at the time, especially Loretta Lynn and Dolly Parton. I think because Loretta Lynn had come up right down the road from my gramma, it made her seem "possible." I don't think that I ever ended up sounding like Dolly or Loretta, but they were always at the forefront of my mind, part of an illumined lineup of everyone I idolized, alongside artists like the Egyptian singer Umm Kulthum and the Lebanese mega-star Fairuz that I had recorded off the radio in high school; Catherine Ringer of the incredible French band Les Rita Mitsouko; the Sugarcubes, who were the most interesting and melodic thing I'd ever heard; as well as my punk rock heroes like Kim Shattuck.

Around this time I had stockpiled a lot of song ideas and poetry, so I decided I should maybe try to make a record of my own. I already had a relationship with Randy and Bill at Mint Records, as they had put out Maow's record as well as Cub's and many other friends'. We all knew each other socially and were regulars in each other's lives. It was the obvious choice. So one day I went into the office and proposed a solo album. To my delight they said yes. Now that I had a chance to make an album, I decided it would be a country album. I somehow persuaded Brian Connelly to come from Toronto and act as a producer. Brian played in one of my favorite bands, Shadowy Men on a Shadowy Planet; he's also one of those people who, even after a long, stellar career, still emanate a constant amazement with music. I knew him to be supportive and kind, and so I repaid this kindness by asking that he sleep on my too-short couch and take the bus with me back and forth to the Miller Block Studio every day to record.

I felt an electric current jagging through me the whole time we were recording, like the days had taken on an extra wattage. This project was mine to steward, and through the management of it, I developed a secret relationship with myself, one I had never experienced before. I had opinions about the sounds and gobbled up technical terminology like it was a meal I'd been starving for all my life. Every day, it seemed, a different musician I admired was in the studio, helping me. Carl Newman came in to play guitar. Carolyn Mark, with whom I had formed a duo harmony-singing band called the Corn Sisters, came to sing. The Corn Sisters came from a dream I had where Carolyn and I were wearing state fair beauty queen sashes and using tap shoes as percussion. We made it a reality and had many adventures together. Matt Murphy from the Super Friendz and the mandolin master John Reischman joined in with local luminaries like the drummer extraordinaire Pete Bourne and the bassist Kevin Beesley-Hammond.

I flew along, high as a hummingbird, sustained by the music and my roommate and best friend Robynn Iwata's chocolate chip toffee cookies, riding sugar and incredulity. At times I'd look around the studio and simultaneously feel crushed and moved that these people were here, in the room with me, pitching in and willing to be a part of something I was creating. I experienced myself as so unlovable, and yet around me were these encouraging examples of love and affection—it was at once shattering, heartbreaking, and exhilarating. Fear and adrenaline remained at the core of my being, but still, emboldened by my comrades, I made intrepid moves. I put a cover of Queen's "Misfire" on the album, and recorded a song by Scott Walker, "Duchess," which was so out of my depth it's frightening to look back on. I had decided I would make country music, and there I was, making it.

It was only later, after I'd recorded a couple of albums, that my Gramma Mary Ann confided that she had once sung harmony in a country band with her brother, Edwin. They played one of the same little places Loretta Lynn had supposedly played, "'cause she had only lived twenty minutes away in Custer."

Why had she not told me this story before? What about this story *wouldn't* interest me? It was so shocking! And not shocking. As soon as she told me about being in a band, I remembered her sweet voice when we drove around in her electric-blue Vega, singing along to the country station on the AM radio. It was very soft, almost shy, but there'd been something beautiful and true in it. I inherited my love for country music from her, and now I knew there was an inheritance of making music, too.

Chauncey and I were still dating in the months after *The Virginian*'s release, and there was a feeling during this time that if I playacted hard enough, I could shape the universe to my will. I could make music. I could be in a long-term relationship with someone who *also* made music. If I had once been a kid too shy to sing outside the confines of her bathtub, now here I was, with an album where I sang all by myself—song after song after song. I ignored that I was operating on sheer adrenaline and that deep down, I was still very afraid. I was walking the plank off a pirate ship, frantically nailing down boards, one after another after another, so I wouldn't fall into the sea.

About a year and a half after the first album came out, in 1997, a major label came a-rap, rap, rapping on my chamber door. Picture it like something out of a fairy tale: There's a knock at the door, a fascinating stranger stands outside, and they want to grant you all your wishes! It's happening—it's happening, Cinderella, look on up—you're going to the ball.

I was flown to LA. I was taken CD shopping, treated to dinner. There was even a facial in Hollywood! Promises glinted through the air, but I was the one making them—I had this idea that now, with this deal, I was going to have enough money to finally be safe from something I couldn't put into words.

My heart kept fluttering like it had wings.

Then the deal fell through.

Of course it did!

Chauncey had dumped me for someone else not long beforehand. We were together for years and then, after one short phone call, it was over.

I'd been so high making *The Virginian,* and now I had skidded so low.

I couldn't take it. It was so unfair and humiliating. I was loud and pissed off about it, my heart so broken that I raged and raged until eventually everyone I knew was angry with me.

And then I wasn't the fairy-tale kid who got it all, but just some broke asshole with half a heart and no art degree.

That's when I found out that you really, really can't outrun the past. No matter how much you think you can. I felt a hot molten shame, like for a few years I'd fooled everyone into thinking I was some sort of human-shaped person with a future only to be found out for what I was: a janky beast, going nowhere.

And I hadn't even hit bottom yet.

There's a neighborhood in Vancouver called Shaughnessy. It's where the *very* rich people live, and to call it a neighborhood doesn't seem right, since that makes it sound like there might be activity in it. And I never—not once—saw a person there. Never saw a car in a driveway. Never heard voices or a dog bark. Never even saw an errant cat lolling in the grass or prowling along the bushes. You know how you can go past a house and somehow know it's empty? That's what the houses in Shaughnessy were like. They were still and quiet as mausoleums. What did live there, though, was a lush forest of enormous trees and bushes of creeping ivy and prickly hedges. The trees were especially beautiful, with witchy old trunks. It was this neighborhood that I'd cut through on my way to school that spring.

I could have caught a bus—the 16 stopped right outside my apartment on Oak Street—but I preferred to walk. I was falling apart. I could feel it, a constant unease in my bones that kept me moving, too deeply agitated to stand still. No one was talking to me. My bandmates were avoiding me. Chauncey didn't want to speak to me, and why would he? He had someone new to forget me with. My best friend, Robynn, was halfway around the world, in Egypt. Her brother and my dear friend, Randy Iwata, who ran Mint Records (the label that released my first solo record, *The Virginian*), had moved into her old room, and at night he and I sat together watching TV, a little pool of companionship, but otherwise the days wrenched by, comprised of solitary walks to and from school through the empty forest of Shaughnessy. In fairy tales someone is always hurrying to get through the woods before dark, and that was how I was living, except I would silently wish for the darkness. It was spring and should have been a radiant time of year, but I was always scurrying along in some gray half-light, dusk coming fast around me.

Two years before I'd been so full of hope. I'd been in love with my classes at school. With making music with friends. I'd made my own album, and I knew I wanted so badly to make more. I was playing shows and writing songs. I had my fingers crossed that it was only a matter of time before I broke through to the next level, whatever that meant. If I didn't have a family I could count on, that didn't matter because my boyfriend did.

When Chauncey and I were dating, we'd hang out for days at his parents' house with that Currier and Ives print of the picnicking family sitting beside Niagara Falls on the wall, and we'd eat dinner at the table, and I would feel this warm contentment running through me. The talk would be so gentle and easy, the food so good, it seemed in those moments like I had successfully outrun every shadowy, shitty part of my past. There was nourishment now. Like I had gripped the earth with my long, half-werewolf toes and run so hard that I'd successfully whirled my way out of my old life and into this new one. I'd become a part of the warm circle that sits around a table in a cozy little house while the wind howls outside, and the rain comes down in never-ending sheets, but it doesn't matter because you're on the inside, warm and fed and loved. His was the kind of family I'd dreamed about being a part of when I was a kid, when I'd be waiting for endless hours in front of the TV for my dad to come home, or on the front porch, hungry and bored, on the lookout for my mom and stepdad, and I loved them with all my heart.

And now here I was, alone again. Someone who no one wanted to talk to. Someone who everyone was pissed at or avoiding for different reasons. All my confidence was gone. All my hope was, too. There was only a new, but familiar, desperation. My blood flowed coarse and sluggish. All I could think of was how close I had been—*so* close—to what I wanted. It was a brutal, lonely place to be.

Chapter 16

Predators

It was around this time that I started to become aware that a man was following me. I would sense him trailing behind me as I went to my classes. If I went to the window of my room on Oak Street, I'd know he was down there, looking up at the building. I still walked to school, but I started looking over my shoulder. One morning, walking down the sidewalk, I saw movement and stopped, not just in fear but out of the pure shock of seeing something alive in the sterile, posh neighborhood of Shaughnessy. A gray figure emerged amid the green, cocky and casual. A coyote. The animal looked right in my eyes like it recognized me. Like I was its kin. An opportunist garbage feeder knows its own kind, after all. Or was it the timeless trickster god finally showing themself to me, letting me know I'd been had? *How cruel.* I already knew anyway!

Soon after, there was a message on the answering machine one night when I got home from classes: "Rick is dead." Rick McGrew was a friend from Tacoma, the beloved old boyfriend who gave me my first drum kit. It was three janky thrift-store drums—a bass drum and two toms—and a crappy ride cymbal, but such a huge deal to me. After we broke up, we remained friends. Friendship was our real mission. Rick was one of those people who glue others together and make people feel good about themselves, a gravitational center among our circle of friends. He loved to play guitar and had lots of old blues records.

I had always known Rick had a little money, more than was usual for Tacoma, and one time when he, our friend J.P., and I were hanging out, he told us the story of his family and the reason why he got some cash every month. His grandfather had been responsible for getting rubber tires into the woods for Weyerhaeuser, the clear-cutting timber lords of the Pacific Northwest. Before, trucks hadn't been able to get across the forest soil; then, thanks to Rick's grandfather, they could, allowing the Weyerhaeuser corporation to deforest massive tracts of land that much faster. For as long as I could remember, I'd been cognizant of the ugly scars left by clear-cutting and who was responsible for them. Rick looked ashamed of this bit of family history. "Someday," he said, "the forest is going to have its revenge on my family." At the time, I understood this the way young people do—half believing and half feeling the wire crack in my body that said fate was something that could be outrun and outwitted. Now this message on my answering machine: "Rick is dead." I heard the words, and then in the shock of it just kept listening to the other messages, standing there in my little rust-colored bedroom on Oak Street, like nothing had happened.

Later, I contacted J.P., and he told me that Rick had been killed in a car accident. Rick and three others, including his son and his uncle, had been crushed in the cab of his truck by a massive tree falling in a windstorm. A motorcyclist behind them described the scene of the accident as "eerily quiet." All four people in the truck had died on impact. The forest had taken three generations of his people in seconds. I couldn't digest the news, only vaguely feeling my tectonic plates grinding out of place. I'd never lost a friend like this before.

In my imagination, Rick remained the same young person he'd been when I first knew him in Tacoma—a tall guy with curly hair falling in his face, generous, musical, with an intelligent, roving mind. Before I left Tacoma he'd partnered up with a woman everyone knew was trouble. She had a young daughter who he'd sometimes bring to see me when I worked at the Java Jive. He and the woman had had a son together as well, and when the relationship busted up, he'd left his stepdaughter behind. I never said anything to him about it, but it bothered me so deeply—I had been that little girl left behind, too.

I still loved him. Time hadn't eroded that. And because I was already creeping through the world with so much unease and fear, I registered Rick's death with superstitious dread. It felt like the bad things I'd left behind in Washington had followed me here. One of my best friends from home was dead on top of every other terrible thing that had happened; what would be next?

I only had one semester of school left. I was having a hard time working up any of my old excitement for college, but there were two classes I liked: electronics and bookmaking. For electronics, we were given the assignment to build a mechanized object. I built a toy rabbit. Not just any old toy rabbit—I wanted the rabbit to look like it'd been designed by a monster to lure a human child. I constructed it from green faux alligator skin and red fake fur, reasoning that a monster who lived under the bed would only have a very vague idea of what a rabbit looked like. It was rigged to lie on its side, and when picked up, a mercury switch hooked to a battery set off a piercing car alarm. All these elements were housed in a plastic Coke bottle inside the rabbit; a bulky, Frankenstein-stitched zipper around the rabbit's neck allowed access. The idea was that once the alarm was bleating, the monster could emerge to snag the child and eat it, I guess?

That was how my mind was working that spring. I was the monster under the bed, and also the child who would be trapped. I was the inventor at the monster's toy factory, and I was a girl who was being followed wherever she went by a man who wanted to hurt her. Except as the weeks went on, I knew this man didn't just want to hurt me, he wanted to kill me. And worse than that, he wanted to rape me. At night, I'd lie in bed listening for his footsteps, hoping to hear the sound of Randy's key turning in the lock so that someone else would be in the apartment, too. I knew then I'd be safe. At school, I'd look over my shoulder expecting to see a sinister face. Every day walking through Shaughnessy, I waited for the man to step out from behind one of the old, witchy trees. Sometimes I wished he *would* show himself, so that the dread would stop and I could actually fight him. Because that's what I planned to do. I would fight. I would rip and bite and tear into him, and I would take him down.

But no one ever stepped out from behind a tree. No one showed themselves. Just once another coyote prowled nonchalantly by, regarding me for a second, unafraid, like a coworker from another part of the monster's toy factory.

My final project for bookmaking was an accordioning book with a white poster board cover and some gold leafing. In it I wrote messages to this man.

HELLO, RAPIST.

I AM DANGEROUS.

IF YOU TRY TO HURT ME, I WILL DESTROY YOU.

I HAVE A KNIFE AND I WILL KILL YOU WITH IT.

TRY IT. I DARE YOU.

GOODBYE, RAPIST

I turned it in and, as I left the classroom, I felt great satisfaction knowing that the book was there on my teacher's desk. I knew the man would come in to look at it, and he'd read my messages. And if he came after me, he'd know that I meant every word I'd written. I would take a knife and I would kill him. I had teeth, thick fur, and eyes that pointed forward on the front of my skull. I was a predator, too.

But then, walking home, I began to feel things closing in. I was shaking. A pressure behind me pushed me up rainy Granville Street toward Shaughnessy. I felt mildly safer among the mansions and the tall hedges, like I was somehow protectively related to the midnight greenness. As I finally drew close to my apartment building on Oak Street, I panicked. The man wasn't at school. He wasn't following me. He was already in the building, waiting for me inside the apartment. Sitting at a table with his dark weapons.

I ducked onto a side block and went to a pay phone at the Safeway up the street. I called Randy at work. "Can you please come?" I was crying.

"I'll be right there," he said, and he was. Twenty minutes later he met me near the front door, and we went upstairs together like soldiers. He unlocked the apartment and, armed with half a curtain rod, strode toward my bedroom. It was incredibly brave. I followed along behind him, trembling.

He opened the door to my room. No one there.

His room. No one there.

No one in the closets.

With the curtain rod raised in his hand, he pushed open the bathroom door. No one there.

As I was walking along behind Randy through the apartment, something strange happened. Standing so near him, it became possible for me to see what was happening through his eyes. I could see that each room of our apartment was empty, with no unhinged man standing in it, and as I absorbed this, reality came shimmering back in, accompanied by a warm little Novocaine sensation. The deep menace I'd felt the past weeks that had me convinced a monstrous rapist was following me as I went to my classes, and standing outside our apartment building at night? I'd made it up. Oh, I thought. Oh. I don't quite know how to describe it, except it was like having a fever break. Or waking from a nightmare. I'd known I was breaking down, but I hadn't comprehended the full extent of it. But I could see it now, see how my depression had crossed over into a kind of psychosis. Randy could see it, too. Very gently he hugged me, and then with absolutely no fuss he put down the curtain rod and, because he knew I was OK now, went back to work.

That book I turned in for class, with all the messages to the killer? I got an A. My teacher never asked me a thing about it.

The bubble had burst. I realized I'd had some sort of psychotic break, but it didn't really alarm me. Mostly what I felt was relief. I figured it was over and I could walk away from it now, like getting up and leaving the theater because the movie's too violent. The human brain doesn't work that way, of course, nor does the world, but that's what I told myself. At least I didn't feel ashamed. Yet.

It was maybe a night or two after this that I ran into a friend at a show. He was going through a painful breakup, too, and his girlfriend was a pal of mine. We ended up hammered and sleeping together, an accidentally well-timed train wreck. I suppose I figured almost everything was ruined, so I might as well take it all the way.

The next day we agreed it was very stupid and there was no reason to tell anyone. Not that anyone was talking to me anyway. We weren't interested in each other romantically, and it had merely been a way to momentarily poke through the tension and sadness that had been separately crushing us both. There. Done. Tidy and sensible. But, in some fit of sadness or desperation, he decided to tell his ex-girlfriend. Perhaps he wanted to make her jealous? I have no idea. I went from someone to avoid to someone to hate in seconds. When I tried to apologize, she wasn't having it, and I don't blame her. She wasn't ready. And I don't know that I was ready yet to understand what I'd been doing, either—the ways I was bent on shredding my entire life, neatly, tidily, and in so doing had shredded a piece of hers. Years later we'd make up, and I'm still grateful to her for allowing me to fuck up then extending me a little grace in the end.

I got through the rest of the spring semester and went to Toronto, just wanting to be with my music friends. I had flamed out in Vancouver, and my way of coping was to relocate, if just temporarily, to the next city. I was the person who left. It's what my family had done when I was a kid, and it felt so familiar, even primal. I would just split open down the back like a small cicada and move on, leaving a dry little amber husk behind in my place. If there was some unresolved feeling in the air, they could talk to the husk, which would slowly erode over time. I didn't do this by choice. I had such little agency over being this way in the world. I just knew instinctively that I couldn't survive if I took all of myself to wherever I was going. This meant I always left a place as an incomplete person, but it was the only way I could see forward. Each time I left I was sure I was moving toward something better, but what I can see now is that I was just moving toward uncertainty.

I had a sort of invisible reek of sadness and low self-esteem that kept people far away, like a sulfuric stink cloud that I emitted into the air around me. Still, there were bright spots, even then, and they revolved around making music with my friends. I was closest to Carolyn Mark, so I joined her in Toronto, and it was a season of festivals and summer legs dusty with mica-flecked dirt, Montreal-style bagels with tomatoes and cucumbers, iced tea, and drinking on warm, starry nights.

We continued our wanderings when we were both back in BC, driving ourselves around as our band, the Corn Sisters, having drinks with every Canadian musician who indulged in such things. I began to forget all the sad husks of myself I'd left scattered behind me. Carolyn's van was named Tony, and for one trip we drove it through the Canadian Rockies all the way from Victoria to Edmonton. Our friend J, who is a performance artist, came along as well. We made a happy trio. Being with these two women was good medicine. I revived around them, once again becoming a little terrier with enough fight to rip the pant leg off a cyclist. We drove and drove and drove.

When we showed up at the home of a friend of Carolyn's named Ian, we were exhausted. It was the middle of the day, but I was ready to go down like a sack of bricks. Ian generously offered me his own bed to nap in, and so I hopped into my pajama pants and wedged myself over his top sheet but beneath his velvety fleece blanket. A song started to play in the other room, so gentle and so simple and so smart. This was the first time I ever heard the music of Ron Sexsmith. His album *Other*

Songs had just come out, and Ian was playing it for Carolyn. I lay there transported, crushed under a thick velvet sea. I cried and wondered at Sexsmith's incredible musicianship and songwriting. The album was gorgeous, like a delicate Swedish snowflake Christmas cookie. His music was a benchmark, a place to aim for. Not to compete with, but to be inspired by. Loving someone else's art can give you a ride at least halfway to where you are trying to go. Even if you don't know where that is yet.

And then we were off and driving again under blue prairie skies, feet on the dash or hands glued to the wheel. Always talking about something we were gonna do, or who we had to meet up with. Carolyn lives her life in the present, and her way of being in the world influenced me greatly. I was so restless, which she helped me see without ever saying a word. Highway driving yields its own kind of linear joy—there is nothing to do but shoot forward along it. There was browsing for hours in thrift stores in Red Deer that smelled pleasantly like old camping gear. Breakfast with the Shenkarek sisters at their restaurant, Cafe Mosaics in Edmonton. Learning about Lhasa de Sela and having cola for breakfast and eating fried green onion cakes. Beers at the Black Dog with Irish Sue, staying at Craig's big yellow house in Calgary and laughing until we cried. Dancing with Blue Rodeo on the bar. And more driving. Always more driving. Big grain elevator buildings holding their own against the sky, colored in line with their *massive* provinces: Alberta green-blue, Saskatchewan and Manitoba rust, gold, silver, and light gray. Fluorescent yellow fields of canola and giant round bales of hay that looked like someone was taking up the carpet of the earth and about to make off with it. Black tattletale phone lines running over the horizon, always faster than you. All the way to Cape Breton.

It was a reprieve from brokenness, and then it was over. I had to face it. With no visa on the way—no record deal, no school, no job—I wasn't going to be able to stay in Canada any longer. I was leaving in total defeat. I had lost my love and my home and myself. I didn't even graduate after all that hard work. I was crushed, and all I could see were the sad little broken husks that trailed behind me that I had tried to forget. I was coming back a bona fide loser. I'd tried for something big and I'd failed. That's how it felt: *You tried, you failed. It's over now. Get back to the back of the line where you belong.*

I gathered up my various piles of junk from the different places I'd lived over the past four years, packed them into my beloved GMC van, and rattled back across the border.

I was heading to stay with my Gramma Mary Ann and her husband, Clyde. They were still in their little butter-yellow farmhouse in the Mount Baker hills. Almost as soon as I pulled into their driveway, I started to shake with fever and aches. It was an epic case of the flu, like I realized I'd dragged myself to somewhere where it was safe to fall apart. I spent a feverish, blurred week in my grandmother's robin's-egg-blue guest room, the nubs of the brown textured carpet like coals under my flu-sore feet as I heaved myself to the bathroom and back. Eventually, I got well enough to join her and Clyde for meals. I liked watching her move around her kitchen. She'd make me toaster waffles, or American "goulash," which was hamburger, tomato sauce, white onions, and elbow macaroni cooked together in a frying pan. When my grandmother spoke about my mom (now living in Alaska with another new and terrible husband), her voice would take on a different tone than her normal, gentle one, like she was mad at her, but wasn't going to tell me why. During the day, we'd sit quietly together and she'd open a trusty Harlequin Romance novel. She read them by the thousands. She spent *years* of her life inside those tiny paperbacks. As my grandmother read, she'd rock herself in her chair—all the women on my mom's side of the family would rock themselves. When I was a kid, my mother used to do it in her bed to fall asleep. My aunts did it. Even while stirring a pot on the stove! That was the way of my mom's family—to rock yourself and stay silent about all the things you weren't naming.

In the mornings I started cinching myself into a pair of big, cumbersome boots and taking long walks through the snow. My grandmother's farmhouse wasn't far from the farmstead where she'd lived with my Ukrainian grandfather, raising my mom and her siblings. There was a limestone quarry nearby, too, and I'd churn through the snow to where the railroad tracks used to be when it was active. Back in the day it had been crawling with men working and railroad cars filling with limestone. My grandpa had worked there; so had Clyde. Now, all up and down the limestone road was deathly quiet. The quarry was just an empty building cropping out of a tunnel in the hill face above, naked and deserted, dusted with snow. Development was what was coming next, like a curse that has an odor you can taste. Already I could see huge boulders that had been placed in front of dirt roadways where they intended to bulldoze all the small, bright pine and birch and fir trees to make housing developments. Little saw-whet owls turned their heads all the way around to watch me walk by, their amber eyes almost too big for their small bodies. I cried for them and the trees. I cried for the Nooksack people who were kicked off this land and all the people who had no fucking idea what bulldozers they themselves were. All those far-flung, terrified idiots who didn't know until they decided it was too late to care about their fellow humans. I cried for Rick, who I still saw as having paid the price for his family. And then there was my family—what ghosts lingered there, what curses, what costs to pay?

I'd walk to the old farmstead where my mother had grown up. I had been in the general area before but had never come to look. Now I visited every day. All that was left was a tall pile of rocks of various sizes that my mother and her siblings had picked from the fields to aid the plows. It was about ten feet tall and six feet wide. I'd stand there in the snow, studying it, picturing my mother in her bandanna carrying rocks over to add to it. It was a tombstone, but still alive. All those rocks could cascade down if they so chose. Or if the mountain chose. Mountains live with a different kind of time than we do, and I cried for that also.

I knew things now that I hadn't known when I was a little kid. I knew that my mother, the girl who had worked in these fields, carrying her rocks across the farm, her hair the shade of a doe's under her bandanna, had been raped by her father in a milking barn on this land. This knowledge circulated in me like its own kind of sluggish blood. When I had met my grandfather years before, he had been a two-dimensional pencil drawing of a man, cursed to fade from then on until he was quietly extinct. This old farmstead was just ours now (whoever *we* were), no longer his. Knowing what my grandfather had done took away all his claims here. He wasn't even allowed to keep his memories. And I knew as I looked out at that awkward rocky tower, at the fields being slowly reclaimed by the forest, that I wanted to save it all somehow. To pause it so I could come back when I was remade and care for this place. Heal it. I was a fool. Maybe it was my first real dangerous sentimentality hangover. Life moves. Not like some capitalist calendar of progress, but in every direction, and it doesn't care about us until we *decide* it does. When we decide we are worthy of its notice and are ready to help. I was not worthy. I only wanted to be. And so I stood there in my big boots, and thought about how it wasn't so long ago that the major record company was buying me dinners and plane tickets, and how if they'd signed me, I could have used that money to buy this land and save it, like a stone-cold wizard who comes in and in one magic stroke fixes the world.

Two weeks had gone by, and I suggested to Gramma that maybe I could live there for a while. I imagined helping around the house and getting a job. Continuing to eat dinner with her and Clyde in the yellow and brown kitchen.

"No," she said. Just that. "No."

It wasn't mean or judgmental. She just thought I could do better. I remained her favorite, I knew that. And maybe, who knows, that "no" was what eventually got me here. Maybe she knew it would have been a fatal retreat from any kind of trying. My aunt and uncle, Judy and Jim, were staying at the house, too, and while I was there Jim bought a set of tires for my van. Some little kindnesses stay with you forever. Those tires were like that, and with those new tires, I reluctantly headed to Seattle, like the demolition derby car, Number 26, revving back toward life, looking to be welded back together.

Chapter 17

Changes You Can't See

When I was a kid, I'd squinched closed my eyes with a wild desire for horses, and when I'd opened them, two horses were clip-clopping up the dirt alley. It had been like magic.

There was still a part of me that thought this was how all good things happened, with big strokes from the universe: You were unnoticed and then someone chose you and you were happy forever. Your mom was dead, and then she was alive! You were nobody and then a major record company signed you and you could pay your bills and be happy forever. One strike of lightning and you were transformed. I didn't understand yet that there were quieter ways of good things happening, and that they were already at work in my life, even during times that felt bleak and hopeless.

Good things had started inside me when I was still back in Canada and working on songs.

People often ask me how I write songs. Honestly, there's no one method, so I couldn't walk you through it even if we had all the time in the world. Sometimes lyrics come first, sometimes music. Some songs take thirty minutes to write, others take years. Some are grim chores and others feel like they just fell out of the pocket of a coat I haven't worn in a while, like a slumbering twenty-dollar bill. I can tell you what it feels like *in* the songs, though.

Songs are part homemade diorama, part gerbil maze, and part eighties music video—location, story arc, and cinematic container. You build all the tiny props inside so lovingly and sometimes they just aren't to scale, so you have to start over, and it's crushing. There are tantrums, tears.

Writing a song starts in the middle of a world you haven't invented yet. It's like trying to decide exactly what a city is like based on one postcard with no writing on the back. An impression or phrase builds a little fire of feeling that causes you to react with construction paper and Popsicle sticks and grade-school poetry and Scotch tape. You work simultaneously forward and back from the middle. You must build its container and its atmosphere, and you need to build it so you can live there, too. If you end up keeping the things you make that don't match the scale of the other things it has to be an intentional "stylistic choice." You have to arrive at the answer just shy of "correct." You must be precise by eyeballing it, no measuring. It has to be *exactly* not right. Maybe you stare into it until you have double vision. The ideas, no matter how simple, are tricky and jump around. Like throwing a dart with your eyes closed. You know how to do it, the weight of the dart in your hand, the arc, the direction of the board. But despite all your muscle memory know-how you still may just break a window. You have to build the tools to build the world. It is the finest, most exquisite puzzle that exists, ten thousand times harder than the *New York Times* Saturday crossword. There's even danger. You'd dare not forget your notebook in the pocket of the airline seat in front of you or the world could end. The act of creating a song is the closest I have ever felt to understanding the "place" of your consciousness. You travel to a mind palace in those moments—a landscape you've made, then furnished through memory and invention. It's the cheapest way to travel.

My time in Canada had been formative and turbulent, packed with both exhilaration and defeat, and it was there I first started to find my way to this songwriting place. But the major leap there came just after I left, when I found a tenor guitar. I'd learned about tenor guitars while making my second record, *Furnace Room Lullaby,* in Toronto. I was working at the Gas Station, the recording studio my friends Don Kerr and Dale Morningstar had opened. Up to that point I'd been writing lyrics and melodies, but relied on other people to be the guitar and bass engines behind my songs. It was fun but a little frustrating, as I wasn't always in full control of where my vocal phrasing could go. One day I saw a little Gibson tenor guitar sitting in a corner at the studio. "What the hell is that?" I asked Don. I was in disbelief, almost afraid to ask, because what if it was too good to be true? A small guitar that might fit my tiny hands!? I had tried to play guitar in the past, but I wasn't good at it. I just couldn't spread my fingers apart far enough to make a lot of the chords. The noises I created never sounded particularly musical, which is the reward that keeps you practicing. The last time I'd picked up a guitar I was twenty-two. I was now twenty-nine. The Gibson turned out to be Don's. He's an incredible drummer and singer, and he also played cello, which used the same standard tuning as a tenor guitar. He enthusiastically sang its praises, letting me play it. It was a perfect fit in my hands, and I made a vow that I was going to find one.

When I returned home to Seattle, I went to the Trading Musician, a used-guitar store that a lot of my friends frequented. I hardly had any money, so I needed a cheap tenor, *if* they even had one. They did! It was a ladder-braced Gibson in a fake-denim-patterned chipboard case. As soon as I saw it, I was madly in love. I made a few payments over time and soon it was mine. This was part of the background hum of something decent happening in my life. In the middle of hard times, sometimes we can't see the pieces that are taking shape around us, forming what's going to get us to the next, better, place. We want the big, sudden transformation, the fairy-tale moment that changes everything. But in my experience, that's not how it happens. As time went on, I began to understand in a new way the appearance of the horses when I was a kid—not as something that would swoop in and fix me, but as a force pushing me to keep orienting myself toward the cinnamon scent of what was right and good for me.

When I first arrived in Seattle, I'd called J.P., my oldest friend, and asked if he had any rooms I could rent at his house on Capitol Hill. Luckily he did, but the rub was it would be about a week until his roommate could move out.

I surfed a couple of couches, including my dad's. He was

living in Seattle, just north of Ballard, in an apartment. In some ways he looked the same. He still had wet brown eyes and a brown beard striped with gray. He had lost most of his hair and looked much smaller to me, but he was still my dad. He even still wore the gray striped coat he'd had since I was a baby, and his cowboy hat. He seemed to like me more now without the pressure of having to care for me, and we coexisted across those days like easy roommates. My mom had moved to Alaska, and when I delivered updates on her he received the news like you would a weather report from somewhere you no longer lived. If I tried to bring up past stories, he would shrug and not really engage. But still, we got along, and there was a nice rhythm to that week together. At night, I was reading *Fall on Your Knees*, by Ann-Marie MacDonald. It was the delicious little hard candy lead weight that kept me hovering at the bottom of the murky tank. How bad could it get? The novel tells the story of a miserable family, and one of the daughters of the house, Frances, who is always in trouble but doesn't stop. Frances knows she is "bad" but spits in badness's face. I was trying to take courage from her and her filthy little communion gloves.

I asked my old friend Cyril Barrett for a job at Hattie's Hat, a landmark restaurant and bar in Ballard. All he had available was a dishwasher position, but I wasn't too cool for that, so there I was at the big sinks at the back, soaking wet and prune-wrinkled with a stomach rash from my warm, damp, and angry ambitions smashed inside my tight apron. My dreams thought I was a dick but suffered me anyway as I was trying to hang in there. My dreams pitied me, I could feel that.

The crew at Hattie's made a good temporary family. They understood I was a musician and were flexible about hours.

I mostly worked the night shift with Tiger. Tiger was a lean, butch woman who had come off the streets. She was loud and hilarious. Every time I made her laugh, I felt like I won the Nobel Prize. She had a sweet, sinewy heart.

Another nice thing about Hattie's was that no one expected you to put up with abuse from customers. I earned money to make installments on that first tenor guitar. Pretty soon I was promoted to prep cook and I got to work in the basement cutting endless vegetables and making soup stock. Eventually, as I gained confidence, I ended up inventing some soups that became pretty popular. There was butternut squash, walnut, and rum. Another was turkey, wild rice, and kale with sun-dried tomatoes, which I still make to this day. There was something I liked about feeding someone I might never meet or even see, making sure they were getting a balance of good things in one bowl. That one bowl might be enough to set up their whole day. I wanted everyone to have a chance at one good, solid meal. They might accidentally neglect themselves, but not on my watch!

After my shift, I spent late nights at home with a book or softly strumming my little tenor guitar. I don't think I cooked myself a single meal in that house on Capitol Hill. I just ate tortillas out of the bag. Things were getting better, but I was still sad from the breakup with Chauncey and shaken whenever I thought of my future. The red digital face of the clock glowed across the beige carpet where I slept on the floor on a foam pad, and I'd remind myself that at least I had a room.

My friend J.P. is a lovable, gregarious guy, and when we'd been living in Tacoma, we could talk about music and art forever. His knowledge was encyclopedic. It was great to be back in proximity to him, but our time together was limited. He went to bed at 8:00 p.m. because he was a delivery driver for a juice company and got up at the crack. So mostly I'd hang out with our roommate Brad. Our favorite thing was to watch *Twin Peaks* together. Brad worked in a video store and rationed our viewing to two episodes a night, tops, to keep it delicious. When we finally watched the last episode, we celebrated with some doughnuts.

Not long after we finished *Twin Peaks*, I got an offer to move into the Washington Shoe Building, one of the last live-work artist spaces in downtown Seattle. My friend Matt was living there with his dog Charlotte, and he invited me to move in with them. That dog liked no one but Matt, but I didn't hold it against her; she had had a rough life before kind Matt came along. Matt, who was from St. Paul, was a bartender at the Tractor, a popular bar and music venue that was just a couple of doors down from Hattie's.

The Washington Shoe Building is a very large, brick, turn-of-the-century industrial factory that sits at the corner of Occidental and Jackson in Pioneer Square. There was a good coffee shop downstairs; I was really moving up to have a spot there. I finally had a good space to make art again. Or so I thought. It turned out the building had paper-thin walls and floors, with huge gaps everywhere. You could hear everything everyone else was doing. It *really* sucked, but I could see the Smith Tower illuminated out my window, and looking at it, I'd tell myself that that was good enough, though I secretly remained unconvinced. I should have known when I first saw the free-floating sleep cube made from plywood and mattresses that Matt had built for himself in his room. Not that he ever sugarcoated what the building was like—he'd been very up front—I think I was just so enamored with having space to try to make things again, I refused to see what I suspected might be true.

One of our neighbors was a woman named Chai, who lived directly downstairs from our place. She had a "gallery" she called "Gallery Chai," where she turned tricks all day very loudly. Lots of her johns were really violent sounding, and if you got tired of listening to them grunting away like someone was having their head smacked in, too bad. If I banged on the floor, some of her clients would scream that they were gonna kill me, so I just had to live with it. Music didn't really drown it out. I don't have any ethical or personal problem with sex work, or people's consensual kinks, it's just that some of the noises, the violent sound of the commerce going down, made me want to get as far away as possible. Then there was Chad, who was a fratty, trust-fund jam-band lover with big speakers and a swing in his living room. I knew about the swing because he left his door open a lot. He cranked the stalest jams with the loudest bass that would vibrate you right off the toilet seat. Nowhere was safe.

Matt told me the story of the zenith of Chad's stupidity. The Washington Shoe Building has a huge round wooden water tower on the roof. One night, as Chad pushed some mushroomed-up hippie damsel to and fro on his swing, he had the bright idea of taking her swimming. How genius! How romantic! They somehow got up through the roof hatch and climbed the iron-runged ladder up the side of the tank like they were born to it. Luckily the phrase "ladies first" didn't occur to the unchivalrous Chad and he jumped inside, hogging all the glory for himself. Since there had been no water in the tower since the sixties, Chad lay on the bottom of the very dry tank with a freshly broken leg. Your tax dollars enabled the helivac paramedics to get him out on a cleverly rigged orange stretcher from the sky.

By then, my beloved GMC had given up the ghost and I was driving a Ford Club van that was a primer blue and had mismatched bench seats bungeed into place. When I got home from work, I'd have to park it by the 99 freeway overpass, which would have been fine except the drug addicts who roamed the area slashed your tires, then wanted five bucks to help you change them. There was also the matter of people breaking in to smoke crack in the van. They would always leave the door ajar, a window broken, and the stench of burning shit and piss (that's what crack smells like, for those not in the know) hard smeared into the interior. I'd clean the van and drive with the windows down for days, but there was really no getting rid of the odor. The Washington Shoe Building was turning out to be a fairly exhausting and expensive place to live.

One day I took a friend to the airport, and as I pulled into a spot back home my van expired. That trip was its final kindness, and I didn't blame it. I've never liked Ford vans for distance driving, but this one had a special place in my heart. It was not a workhorse, but it had gotten me home. "Thanks, buddy. You are released," I said softly.

Taking the bus on rainy nights from Pioneer Square to my job in Ballard was sketchy, and I could tell my coworkers at

Hattie's were getting irritated with my requests for rides back into downtown Seattle at the end of the night. It was time to find a new van. I borrowed three thousand dollars from my record company, Mint Records, and got right to it.

But I needed a wingman. Who better to go van shopping with than my dad, the guy who knew everything about automobiles? So one Saturday we hit the used-car strip on Aurora Avenue. Dealership after dealership, we came up empty. At one, I was talking to a salesman about a Club van on the lot. I'd liked my first, and this one was red and white and clean looking. My dad got under the hood as the salesman and I talked.

"It's four thousand dollars," he said.

I swallowed. That was five hundred dollars more than I had.

My dad appeared at the side of the van holding up the dipstick to show a solid silver strip.

"There's no oil in this engine," he said matter-of-factly. "Let's go."

The salesman's jawbone liquefied and emptied down the front of his neck.

The lesson I learned: Always check the obvious, even if it's kind of embarrassing.

My dad and I had had a really hard relationship my whole life, but since I had become a semi-adult and shown I could hold down a job and go to college we got along OK. He no longer had to raise me. Not that he'd done much of that before. I had been something my mother had saddled him with— a burden, a distraction, a roadblock. But now we were talking about vans, our shared wheelhouse. We were just a couple of guys shopping for a decent vehicle. It wasn't all that different from those weekends years before when I'd worked on the white Buick Special in Blue's backyard.

We had pretty much given up and were headed back south toward my dad's place when I saw it: a dark brown rectangle shape toward the back of a lot.

"Look!" I cried.

He pulled into the driveway of a dealership we had missed in our earlier trawl of the strip. It came into view: a half-brown, half-silver GMC Rally STX 6.2 diesel van, the color of a Hershey Bar wrapper and gorgeous. It was in perfectly well-loved shape and the exact size I wanted, a twelve-passenger with bench seats and barn doors. The former owner had even built a custom wooden drink holder on the front console to accommodate extra-large coffee mugs. I was home. The interior was a golden-brown vinyl and cloth. It passed my dad's tech inspection with flying colors. It cost me thirty-five hundred dollars and was the best money I ever spent. Diesel was cheap back then, and it had a thirty-three-gallon tank. I could cross three states in that sweet van on one tank, no problem. The van would eventually be known as "The Beaver" in honor of its brown color and its having been built in Ontario. I have never had a deeper relationship with a vehicle before or since. My dad helped me put a used tape deck in and I was good to go.

Not long after the van-buying expedition, my dad lost his job. He was an exceptionally skilled draftsman by this point, but a strange, quiet man, and I suspect he made his bosses uncomfortable. He had always been depressive, and the drinking made it worse—it made him seem secretive, inscrutable. Even as his daughter, I didn't know him much better than his colleagues did. He came across as a shy guy, always hiding behind a cowboy hat, who seemed disappointed in himself. Now, I saw a new, deeper sadness come over him. He'd held down a full-time job his whole life and felt thrown away. I didn't know it then, but this trip together along Aurora, talking vans and shooting the breeze, two dudes cruising the car lots, was the last normal thing we'd ever do together.

Around this time, I went to Chicago to visit my friends Ben Schneider and Rob Miller. During the day I sat in their house and wrote my first-ever song by myself, called "Favorite." Before that I had worked with many players to help me shape the songs, which would look like me singing a melody into the air and the bandmate helping figure out the chords underneath. Darkish and tongue-in-cheek, "Favorite" was based on a dream I had where I had a relationship with fate and it chose to spare me some horrible outcome, but not others. In the dream I'd felt guilty, but I kept running and running and not looking back. As the song took shape, I could feel something new splitting open in the world. It was like suddenly going from being completely stranded to having a car and knowing you can leave anytime you want, that you can *go* anywhere you want. It was freedom.

Rob was the co-owner of Bloodshot Records, and he said we should put the song on a compilation they were releasing. I got Tom Ray to come play bass, and Jon Rauhouse (who was in town for some reason; he normally lived in Phoenix) to play pedal steel. It was sounding good, so I asked Brett Sparks from the Handsome Family (I was and still am a monumental fan of theirs) to sing on the bridge. I sang and played my tenor guitar.

As soon as I heard the song played back to me, I loved it. I still do. I was so proud to have played guitar on a song I wrote. It was also the beginning of what would become a long and happy relationship with Tom and Jon as my principal bandmates. I'd go on to write many songs by myself, but it got a little lonely, so I started writing with Tom and Jon on occasion. Then Paul Rigby. I never wanted to play music to be a solo musician, I wanted to be *in a band*! In a gang. In a pod. *In* it. I wanted camaraderie and adventure, and I did not want to go it alone. I still don't. That trip to Chicago had all the seeds of what was coming.

Back in Seattle, Matt and I continued to work our dueling bar and restaurant shifts and did our best. I spruced up my room, even painted it. And then the news came: the building was going condo. All of us tenants had exactly three weeks to get out before it was overrun by genetically hindered French bulldogs and their owners.

Three weeks is not a lot of notice, and many people had a lot of trouble locating where they'd go next. On the last day before the eviction deadline, there was a huge line at the building's single freight elevator as everyone loaded up their things. We all helped each other, a community spirit animating the proceedings. You had to have your vehicle lined up outside at *just* the right point to meet the elevator to get your stuff out. Outside the building there were lines of vehicles of every shape and size, and lines made of humans and all their possessions snaking down the hallways inside the various floors of the building. The scene looked like settlers waiting on a train platform to meet the wagons that would take them down the Santa Fe Trail.

Finally, there were just a few of us left when Chad and some frat buddy of his cut the line and somehow took control of the elevator.

"Robin Hood!" Chad whooped, and his friend whooped back, "Robin Hood!"

No one complained, and I think I know why. It was because every person in that building knew Chad was a full-on choad. They let him go just to be rid of that idiot. We couldn't even be bothered to hate him, which is how, I suspect, a lot of spoiled white men get away with so much in this world.

I said a fond farewell to Matt and Charlotte the dog and loaded the Beaver and lit out for Chicago. I was done with the humiliation of the Northwest. My friend Lyle had agreed to help me drive. Lyle isn't much of a talker, and we were having a very peaceful trip. We were happy with the stereo glow lighting up our faces with the Handsome Family's baritone storytelling and drum machine clicking off the miles. Their original murder ballads and bizarre, funny tales kept us buzzing with the energy of "the other side."

One night, in South Dakota, we realized we were near Mount Rushmore and the moon was full. It was a truly gorgeous late-spring night with a balmy breeze. We decided to sneak in. We parked a ways off the side of the road and entered the park on what must have been a game trail. It was dark in the pine trees and we had to squeeze between bushes, and I swear to god I felt a deer's rump brush past my naked springtime arm. It gave me chills. The pine oil from the trees was intoxicating. Before it was stolen from them, this land had been sacred to the native peoples of the Plains, including the Lakota, the Arapaho, and the Cheyenne, and you could still feel why in the air. After blindly battling through the brush, we came out onto the main concrete causeway up to the mountain, named Six Grandfathers (T̆huŋkášila Šákpe) by the Lakota. The moonlight was electric, shining down in judgment on the faces of those white men carved into the sacred mountain by Gutzon Borglum, a known Klansman. Lit harshly from above, their faces looked like skulls. Lyle and I basked in the light bouncing off their condemned features for a while. We were tiny, and tinier still were many of the petty, cruel deeds of those men. It was a wanted poster, not a monument.

We trekked back to the van and drove on.

Chapter 18

Imagine It into Being

I still had a gray, knee-length fake-lambskin coat, pulled from the same box containing the other fake-fur coat in the laundry room of my building back in Vancouver. It was the most appropriate thing I had for that first Chicago autumn. Then came the freezing Chicago winter, with the wind hammering in like a bouquet of cold fists, and that coat was no longer fit for the job, but it was the best I had so I wore it with three sweaters underneath, a big scarf, and a hat. I looked like a stuffed armchair, which got me some looks, but what else could I do? I'd shuffle my ass to the L in all weathers with a huge backpack on. A puffy, gray faux-lambskin mule.

And then it was summer and so hot. SO hot!

My dear friend Judge had found a great apartment on Maplewood Avenue in Humboldt Park for us. It was spacious, with high ceilings, old wood floors, and bizarre pink plastic tiles in the bathroom, of which only a couple had cigarette burns. The two of us set to homemaking with a passion. We painted the living room "Shakespeare Green" and the entry room "Klondike Blue," and then kept on trying other colors until we eventually became the reason that Home Depot no longer lets you return paint. There was a back porch, which was lovely to sit on, and Judge arranged tin cans upside down on sticks in the planters so she could record the beautiful, calming percussion sound of the summer storm rain falling on them.

The apartment had no air-conditioning, which was fine—until it wasn't. An epic heat wave slopped over the city like dirty dishwater. The bassist Tom Ray once described the sensation of being this overheated like this: "My pants feel like five layers of hot lettuce." It's the most apt description I have ever heard. It was so hot that summer, it didn't even cool down at night, and Judge and I became more and more chaotic, the lack of sleep driving us toward the brink of madness. But a window unit in the kitchen fixed us right up, and all was well in the apartment again. We fought our local squirrels, ate bad burritos, drank frosty Cokes, and enjoyed our home together.

Judge had gotten me a job at an animation studio. Meanwhile, she had her own day job and also worked some nights at the Hideout, a great bar and venue in the city, so I often had the apartment to myself. I was working hard on becoming a better guitar player, playing my acoustic tenor for hours and hours. But what I really wanted was an electric tenor. I figured this was the sort of desire that wasn't going to be quenched—who kept electric tenor guitars in stock?—but then I heard from my friend Andrew that he had sighted one at a fancy guitar store over on Damen Ave.

"HOLY SHIT!" I was in love before I even laid eyes on it. All I knew was that it was a Gretsch. I talked Andrew into going to see it with me the very next day.

We walked into the empty store. The salesman asked if he could help. I blurted out that I'd heard about the electric tenor guitar, and I wanted to see it *so* bad. The salesman pulled a face. "Um, that guitar is on hold for Rick Nielsen of Cheap Trick."

The pressure of my disappointment could have shattered the windows. The salesman stood there, looking pleased with himself. Then, right that second, before my heart ceased to beat, a man stood up from behind a shelving unit, like a submarine periscope poking out of the water from nowhere, and exclaimed, "C'mon, he's *never* gonna buy it. Just let her look at it, man!"

It was Tom Petersson, the bassist from Cheap Trick, and I owe him forever. If I could have knighted him there on the spot I would have. The salesman, who turned out to be the store's owner, begrudgingly went into a back room and returned with the guitar.

"It's three thousand dollars," he said, setting the case down. Still pleased with himself but now also irked. He returned to helping Tom Petersson like Andrew and I didn't exist.

We filed into the amp room, and I opened the case. The guitar inside was the most beautiful thing I had ever seen. Ebony black with white binding around the outside, it was worn, clearly loved by somebody. I plugged it in and the magic electric sounds poured out. I was still a very novice player, so I asked Andrew to give it a try so I could see what it could do for real. As he began to play, I was struck by how nice the low end sounded for a guitar with only four high strings. It was gorgeous. The case was an original auburn tweed with a royal red interior. I opened the pocket inside to find a piece of paper, which I unfolded. It was a repair receipt that had been paid for by Ry Cooder. This had been *HIS* guitar!

Now, I knew I would do anything to make this guitar my own, but paying extra once the store owner realized who its previous owner was was not one of them. I deserved a chance, too, dammit! It was already *way* more than I could afford, so I slipped the receipt with Cooder's name into my jeans pocket and never looked back. Months and months of layaway later, it was mine. I slept with it. I played it at Union Chapel, at my first-ever show in London, on my thirtieth birthday (with the glorious Handsome Family). I wrote many of the songs that would appear on *Fox Confessor Brings the Flood* with it. We could do anything together.

Around the time I got the new guitar, Carolyn Mark, my fellow Corn Sister, came to town. It was glorious to have her in the house. Sitting together on the couch of the apartment on Maplewood, we watched the Margaret Cho special *I'm the One That I Want*. In it, Cho talks about being told by network heads that she was "too fat" to play herself in *All-American Girl*, the TV show based on her *own* life. We laughed and we cried.

Watching Margaret Cho raging across the stage, I was beginning to recognize some way of inhabiting the world that was big and defiant and incredibly radiant, too, like allowing all the corners and recesses of yourself, even the weird ones, to become a part of your art. It was deeply inspiring. By the time I moved to Chicago, I'd recorded two solo albums and performed with Maow, the Sadies, and the Corn Sisters; I'd played *tons* of shows, driving in vans from city to city. And I still found it hard to even say out loud the words "I'm a musician." It felt too revealing—who was I to want anything? To have a desire strong enough to pursue it? More than that, it felt like bragging. Somewhere in my inner cells I remembered the shame I felt as a little kid when my mom came in and saw me putting on the bandanna in the mirror and said, "You're going to become vain." Something cold and acid in her voice communicated that was the worst thing in the world you could be. Now, as an adult, I agreed—we all know assholes who brag a lot, and who wants to be one of them? But I couldn't untangle the difference between "bragging" and simply wanting to exist in the world and make music and feel proud of what you do. I've met a lot of people who get confused about this, too, and most often they're women. I had gotten into the habit of making myself small to please my mom, and I didn't know how to outgrow it. But when I watched people like Margaret Cho, I'd see ways you could make things and be in the world but without boasting or apologizing for being who you were. Watching her felt like an invitation, like "c'mon up here with us." It's the way I'd feel reading Lynda Barry's comics. Or listening to the Cramps.

I didn't have it sorted out then. I still don't have it sorted out. But when I look back at the time I spent in Chicago, there was a shift happening, and I know it because when it came time to fill out my taxes, and I had to list my occupation, for the first time ever I put down "musician."

About a year after I'd moved to Illinois I was standing on a stage, and my field of vision was moving inward, the edges blurring. The summer sun was hitting my body like a hammer, and a wave of nausea surged up in answer. None of this was how I expected to feel playing at the Grand Ole Opry.

When my agent called to tell me I'd been asked to play there, I was floored. My Gramma Mary Ann had been a huge fan of the Opry stars all her life. I was so proud and nervous, and I couldn't wait to tell her. When the date finally came, it was the height of the hottest July. Boiling in Chicago and only getting hotter as the band and I crept down the cracked highway south toward Nashville. We were in the trusty Beev, which technically had air-conditioning, but it felt more like having someone's hot breath exhaling at you through some vents. There were five of us packed in there with all our stuff. I was in a loose, large T-shirt and cutoffs just trying to keep it together as we drove.

When we finally pulled up to Opryland, it was ninety-eight degrees and not a cloud in the sky. The sun was punishing, and the humidity swamp-aquatic. Even breathing was hard. I had to steel myself to keep on task as we unpacked the van. "Load-in" was to an outdoor stage right next to a BBQ pit—it was more like we were playing adjacent to the Opry than in it, which was a little disappointing at first but ultimately no big deal. It had a roof but no walls, so the Nashville sun muscled across it at different angles as the day went on, magnetized to the black stage. We did our sound check, then retreated to the air-conditioning of the actual Opry building to get ready for our show. I was still in my orange "Wilderness Pilots Do It in the Bush" T-shirt, which had a cute cartoon beaver with pontoons on his feet. It was just a silly thing, but I was quickly pulled aside and told my shirt wasn't appropriate for the Opry's family atmosphere. I was a little embarrassed. "This isn't what I was gonna wear," I said, a little grossed out by this random employee's seriousness. *I'm not stupid*, I thought. *Yeesh!*

But never mind. As I moved through the building's backstage, I saw Little Jimmy Dickens and Jan Howard. I was starstruck. I was such a fan of both of theirs, and was thrilled to be introduced by our guide. Little Jimmy was gracious and Jan Howard looked at me like I was a piece of sweaty cheese rind. I didn't let it get me down, I was at the Opry to make my gramma proud.

Showtime came and we hit the sweltering stage, the sun now beating directly in front of it. The BBQ pit was smoking full-on like a steam engine. Organ meats sizzling away in the pit, me and my band sizzling away on the black skillet of the stage. I have never before or since been that hot. There was no water anywhere—not a glass or plastic bottle.

I was miserable but trying to keep a brave face, so sweaty that my hands kept slipping off the neck of my guitar. We made it through two thirds of our set and finally I was hallucinating. The world had gone dark in that tunneled way it does when you're about to pass out. That I might puke started to seem more and more like a real possibility. I leaned into the mic and said, "Thank you!" to the audience, calling the break before the encore early.

I knew I needed water—badly. As I reached the exit stairs, a woman barred my path. She looked *very* serious.

"I need forty more minutes up there!" she snapped. I would later learn this was Sally Miller, the Grand Ole Opry's general manager, who had booked me for the show.

"FINE!" I said. I was so thirsty and so mad. I registered

her less as a person and more like a freshly locked gate that was stopping me from getting water. *What the fuck!?*

I staggered back on the stage and, as I walked out, I pulled my shirt over my head. I was wearing a bra, so I wasn't naked, but I also wasn't thinking. It wasn't an act of punk-rock defiance. I just had an animal need to cool down in *any* way possible. The band and I took our positions and began another song (at least I *think* we did?). Soon the power had been cut and I saw the front-of-house engineer laughing his head off.

We were done. I put my shirt back on and guzzled some water that had finally materialized. I was red as a beet. Sally Miller stormed up to me with one of her employees at her side. She did a lot of yelling, which I tried to break up with some "I'm sorrys." I felt so sick and ashamed. She was that kind of mad where I could tell she was enjoying her own righteousness as she shouted away.

Finally, she delivered the classic line, the one we'd both been waiting for: "You'll *NEVER* play this town again!" She stormed away.

We packed up our gear and limped back to the van. Five severely dehydrated musicians. I don't think we even got paid. I was upset that I had let my bandmates down, but they were kind souls and rallied around me. Still, the realization that I'd blown it was as heavy as the air and twice as uncomfortable. When I got back to Chicago, I wrote Sally a long letter of apology explaining that I wasn't trying to be rebellious, I had literally just had *heatstroke*, and that I felt terrible for what had happened. She sent a smug reply to my agent and that was that. I was never going to play that town again. I thought about what men had to do to get banned from the Opry. Hank Williams got booted after missing several shows (this was when he was in his alcoholic slide). Johnny Cash had gotten drunk and, during his show, bashed out all the footlights with his mic. I hadn't been drunk. I hadn't sworn at anyone. I hadn't sent glass flying out at the audience. I'd been overheated and sick. Granted, I wasn't a star and never would be. I was OK with that part, but I was just heartbroken I had blown my shot at playing the Opry. I so badly wanted to do it for my gramma, to make her proud of me.

A few years went by, and I was booked to play the Ryman, which was home to the Opry for decades before it moved over to the Opry House. When I got there, no one looked at me like I was a cheese rind or got in a tizzy about what I might wear onstage. Everyone was friendly and helpful. As my band and I went onstage in that glorious old auditorium, I could feel the magic of playing where so many other musicians I loved had played before. *This* is where it was, not the Christian megapark that had booked me to help sell hot dogs. It was so decent and loving and healing. My gramma had died by then, but I was sure she could feel it anyway. Forever after, I was certain that the institutional cult that's dedicated to deciding what is "country music"—and what isn't—wasn't worth my time. It only exists to exclude people.

No one can stop you from "playing this town again!" or from being yourself or from making dumb, innocent mistakes. No gatekeeper can stop you from playing country music or evolving it past the confines of the tight decades of time they are so desperate to preserve. When it comes to making new things, they can't stop you for being Black or a girl or gay or divorced.

That's the only real "can't"—and don't let them forget it. Just ask Margaret Cho.

One day, in the very early 2000s, while driving across the country, I found myself in lovely Kansas City, Missouri. For years I'd made a point of going through KC on the 70, even though it was slightly south of my route, because it had the best used-record stores. My favorite was Music Exchange (sadly now defunct). I was downstairs, in a side room off the huge main room of the basement. I felt like a monk visiting a vast, private library hidden in a bunker from the German army in World War II. The expansive world below was much larger than the building I had entered.

I decided to peruse the "world music" section, which itself was the size of a small record store. It was meaty. It was there, flipping through albums, that I saw the face of a lady with a huge smile and a gap between her front teeth. It was the first time I ever laid eyes on Yanka Rupkina. She stood with two other beautiful ladies, Eva Georgieva and Stoyanka Boneva, all three women wearing traditional Bulgarian costume. Together, they were Trio Bulgarka.

I went to the listening room to play the album, and I was rapt from the first seconds of the first song. I still am all these years later. Their voices are an emergency, demanding attention. Like an ambulance siren imploring you to "fucking move it or lose it! There's someone dying in here!" But also like a warning that nature is coming to beat your ass. And then cradling you in comfort when no one else will. If you have spent most of your life listening to singing with harmonies in the Western scale, this will turn your head. It might even give you whiplash. It woke something up inside me that day, like the ugly duckling meeting the swan—some understanding about my own voice, and what I'd always seen as its shortcomings (too nasal, lacking vibrato, etc.) slipping into place. Listening to Trio Bulgarka, I could hear how three nasal, loud, un-"pretty" (save maybe Georgieva) swans can disarm you by sounding like a swarm of warm bees and vibrating your core. I felt I had actually *come* from somewhere now, like I had ancestors to hold me up, not just a dead sea with bones at the bottom. It was like they'd handed me a tiny strand of "origin"—a scant red thread that could lead me safely out of the labyrinth.

As a teenager I'd absorbed the idea that to love music meant I'd have to reject the old gods of my childhood—the horses, the myths, the uncanny strangeness. Now here was sonic proof that they could coexist. I closed my eyes and listened, knowing myself in a field, on a steppe with my sisters and our horses, making grasses wave and strangers back away.

Chapter 19

Out of the Old Ashes

Approached from the street, the Louvin Brothers Museum looked like a storefront for an old-timey pawn shop. Back then, in 2002, it sat in the tiny town of Bell Buckle, about an hour's drive outside of Nashville. It sat on the main street, in an old brick building.

My friend Jason had started *Fretboard Journal*, a magazine about all things guitars. Jason was madly in love with tenor guitars, just like I was, and he had asked if I'd write about them. I decided I'd write about *A Tribute to the Delmore Brothers*, a tribute album to the 1930s Opry stars, brothers Alton and Rabon, that the Louvin Brothers recorded back in 1960. I loved the album's simple, heartfelt songs and the lilting close harmony melodies. Their singsong repetition was so addictive. I knew that on that album, Ira Louvin had played Rabon Delmore's old tenor guitar, which seemed like a beautiful piece of musical inheritance.

Calls were made, plane tickets were bought, and I was off to interview Charlie Louvin in Tennessee. To say that I was a *big* fan of the Louvin Brothers doesn't begin to capture it. I had studied their singing for years and years, and I worshiped them. Their close harmonies floated like nasal birds riding a thermal, doing backflips in midair. Holy shit, they could *sing*. Over the decades, they influenced everyone from the Everly Brothers (who are actually even better) to the Byrds to Emmylou Harris, and so many more.

I was accompanied by my boyfriend at the time, Joe. Joe was a luthier (someone who makes stringed instruments) and so, on our way, we stopped by the Museum of Country Music in Nashville, where he could get a load of some of the amazing historic guitars they have on display. I had an appointment with a lovely curator to photograph Rabon Delmore's tenor guitar, which was part of their collection. After getting my pictures, we drove toward Bell Buckle.

I saw Charlie right away, an alert, older man who was on the lookout for us. The museum was so small, he was both the curator and a living part of the exhibit. He told Joe and me to have a look around while he finished up speaking with another visitor. The museum was stuffed, treasures packed in every corner. We marveled over the memorabilia, the sepia-syrup-colored "old days" frozen in brittle photographs. Everyone had beautiful teeth and shellacked hair, their instruments, outfits, and awards gleaming.

Then, while examining a glass case, something caught my eye that jolted me. It was a tiny, novelty pocketknife, silver, but shaped like a man. A man in a hood and a robe. A Ku Klux Klansman. There was no explanation, which was odd considering everything else in the museum was labeled with dates and events or ownership, like "Ira's Cowboy Boots." Something in my chest closed when I saw that knife. The brothers were originally from Section, Alabama; maybe this was part of the culture they escaped? At least that was my justification for it. I wanted to ask, but I had a job to do and I didn't want to fuck it up—for both my sake and my friend Jason's.

Charlie, finished with the other museum visitor, returned to us. I was thinking hard about Joe standing next to me. He was half Puerto Rican. Would there be some weird racist incident? The pocketknife was hot on my mind, and I tried to shove it back down. I had seen my boyfriend harassed by cops after we had been stopped for doing five over in Colorado. They gave him a *really* hard time, claiming it was "suspicious" that we had a box of lemons in the car. But Charlie seemed friendly and warm to both of us, so I brushed my anxieties away.

Joe excused himself to go get something out of the car. I got out my voice recorder, preparing to start the interview. Joe hadn't been gone two seconds before Charlie blurted out, "You sure got big ol' boobs!"

I was so stunned I didn't reply.

My brain was working hard explaining away his comment. Maybe Charlie had Tourette's, and couldn't help blurting things out, and I needed to be compassionate? I felt disgusted, but that, too, I pushed back down. (How do women have any space left inside us with all the shit we swallow?) He acted like nothing had happened. Joe was back now. I did that classic woman move where I figured it was just me. Just like I had done the classic white person move, figuring there was no racism around, either, despite the Ku Klux Klan knife. In other words,

I had shut down all of my gut instincts, hitting some internal "override" button.

I took a deep breath and started the interview, and it was wonderful. Charlie told me many great stories about music and kinship and getting in trouble. None of them seemed racist, thank god. Charlie was forthright about his brother Ira's issues with drinking, misogyny, and rage. It seemed like he must have been the stable one of the pair, and I'm sure that worked in his favor for most of his life. At the close, I felt like we'd had a real conversation and that I had everything I needed for the article. I left semi-shaky but in good spirits.

Back in the car I asked my boyfriend if he had seen the knife. He had, and he also didn't know what to make of it. It was one of those things where you're both scared but also sort of shrug your shoulders, like "I must be misunderstanding this," since there was no further context.

The article came out well, and nine or ten years later I was asked if Charlie and his band could be the special guest on a radio show I was doing in Boulder, Colorado. The question was floated in the air whether I might even sing a song with him.

By then, I had decided I had just been paranoid the first time we met because I had been nervous about the interview. Now, I was headlining the radio show, and we decided that for the finale we would sit in with Charlie for his hit song "Cash on the Barrelhead." I was really excited. Charlie's management gave us the proper key to rehearse on our own and we were off to the races. On the day of the show, we were set to have a sound check rehearsal as well. We all met up onstage and said our hellos. Charlie didn't remember me, but I didn't mind; it had been quite a while since we had met.

Right before the sound check, Charlie announced he was changing the key. It worried me a little. I'm not a trained musician, and it can sometimes be tricky for me to make a key change without time to practice, but I was game. We started the sound check, and I began noodling around in the vocals, trying to find my harmony in the new key.

Charlie's guitar player leaned over to him and said, "She can't sing it."

To be clear, I had *just* started trying. Soon the sound check was over, and I said something like, "I'll woodshed it in the dressing room and get it." No one looked up. You would have thought it was their show and I was just some fuck-up butting in.

I camped in the dressing room, alternatively moping and seething. Then our tour manager Jenn popped in, upset. Apparently, after I had left the stage Charlie had commented on Jenn's ass, and she was fuming. That was it. Together we went to the show's producer and told him our predicament. I didn't want to do the finale with Charlie. The producer felt we were overreacting and beseeched us to "just make it work."

My band and I played our set. It was time now to play the final song with Charlie. My friend Kelly Hogan was there to do harmony vocals, and at the break we stepped into the alley and decided to take a little walk. All these different facts and thoughts circulated in my mind. Charlie's announcement of "You sure got big old boobs" from years ago. The Klansman knife lying in the museum. His talking about Jenn's ass. The way the key change had gone down. The producer's telling us we were overreacting and to "just make it work." How often do women get told that? How often are we expected to tamp our responses back down into our guts?

With Hogan's encouragement, that day I decided "fuck, no" and "no more." I pulled out my phone and called the producer and said, "I'm out." I wasn't going back to sing with that creep or his cunty band. Hogan and I just kept walking through town until we found two giant butterscotch puddings to celebrate our self-emancipation. We had done the right thing and it felt so good.

When Hogan and I returned, everyone was offstage, and we received a crazy report from a gobsmacked Kathleen Judge. Kathleen is our dear friend, my roommate and our merch person, and she told us that Charlie had come out to sell stuff and sign autographs and had casually launched into a racist explanation in response to a fan's inquiry about some specific kind of record. "No! That's n***** music!" he'd exclaimed to the crowd of onlookers and fans.

Our mouths hung open, but honestly, we were not surprised. He was a creep and a racist, just like my instincts had told me. White privilege stops you from listening to your gut, just like patriarchy does, and when that happens, you feel ashamed of yourself and your true heart. It's so very ugly and effective.

While I'll never completely agree with that old chestnut "never meet your idols," I'd now had evidence of how it *can* go really badly. I'd also been able to see how, if someone's a hero to you, you might be willing to overlook lousy behavior and make excuses. Then again, if you never meet at least a few of your idols you never get to have the joyous electric shock of when the person you thought they were from afar turns out to be exactly who they are. Like Mavis Staples up close is just as wonderful and loving as you think she is and Robyn Hitchcock is just that warmly gregarious and funny, to name two. Charlie Louvin didn't live up to what I thought he'd be, but his knuckle dragging didn't mean that other artists aren't worth orbiting closer to.

Months later, the producer of the radio show wrote me an email saying he was very sorry for not listening. I appreciated it, but the whole event was just a big failure in my mind. It didn't help that, before receiving his email, my band and I had finished off a difficult tour with Rufus Wainwright where his tour manager had treated us like absolute garbage. During that tour, we had our trailer stolen, a nasty tire blowout on the freeway, and one million other little things that chipped away at my self-esteem and energy. That night in Colorado was just the low point of a challenging time.

At the end of the tour, I woke up on the bus at about 5:00 a.m. We were on the outskirts of Tucson at the Triple T Truck Stop (one of my favorites) fueling up. I pulled up the black blind in the back lounge to get a look at the fabulous neon "TTT." It glowed in the gray dawn light. It was so early it wasn't as busy as usual, just a few truckers here and there. I noticed one solitary figure. It was Charlie Louvin, smoking a cigarette near a gas pump like a fucking idiot. He was dead a few weeks later.

When I first heard the Flat Duo Jets' music on that traded VHS music video compilation tape belonging to my friend Bill Henderson, it had hit me like a lightning bolt straight out of the TV. It wasn't a romantic lightning but an all-consuming electrocution, an immediate restructuring of my DNA. It took my nervous system and placed it in a sleek new wiring harness. I felt like I had found the gold vein in the granite. I had been switched on.

Fifteen years had passed since then and my love hadn't abated. Not a whit. The music of Dexter Romweber remained my Moby Dick, and I was Captain Ahab, obsessing over the whale I wanted to get close to. But not to destroy it—a crucial difference.

There's an ugliness that can exist in making music—a jealous competitiveness that can infect you when you lack confidence and make you feel like the only way to "win" is for someone else to lose. Back when I'd met Jennifer Finch of L7 at age nineteen, I'd felt that jealousy gnaw at me, and acted crummy as a result. It had nothing to do with her—it was all my own fear. Over time, though, I got better at steering forward—not perfect, just better. A herky-jerky move toward the space I wanted to occupy. And as much as I was able to, it was because I could use the Flat Duo Jets like a navigational star, as something to help me keep an eye on what was authentic and moving to me. Through them, I learned that if you loved something, you didn't have to enact the toxic, masculine principle of destroying the object of your obsession. You could study it, nurture it. You could let your love of Moby Dick turn you into a marine biologist, not a harpooner of beautiful creatures. That slow transformation was the most important of my life.

With each album I made I was able to move further in that direction, further toward pure joy, pure feeling. After *The Virginian* came *Furnace Room Lullaby* in 2000, then *Blacklisted* in

2002—the same year I met Charlie Louvin at his museum and around the same time I first heard the Trio Bulgarka. It was like with each album I was retraining myself how to orient to music that truly moved me.

In 2006, my love for the Flat Duo Jets reached an apex when Dexter played guitar on "That Teenage Feeling," for my fourth album, *Fox Confessor Brings the Flood*. He stayed at my house and we ate Mexican food and hung out on my shaded porch. It was so good to befriend this odd, kind person, to get to know him as a human, not just as a musician whose music had changed me. I could see he was someone who struggled to be at peace in his own body. I couldn't help but feel compassion for it, and recognize it as so familiar a dissonance. He was a funny, self-deprecating, and deeply endearing presence. We bonded over being two people who walk when we are anxious (which is a lot), setting off on long, solitary strolls through cities and countryside.

Fox Confessor also contains the song "Hold On, Hold On." I'd actually written it a couple of years before, in a freezing practice space in Toronto, while working on material for a live record with the Sadies, *The Tigers Have Spoken*. Travis Good, the band's guitarist, had a huge malamute, Wiley, who was taking up the couch and smiling a big smile as the band and I wrote it. The song came together quickly, and it instantly felt right. The B^7 chord made it. Still, it sounded more like a studio track than something for a live album, so I waited to put it out on *Fox Confessor*.

I vividly remember sitting in the bathtub of the apartment I was house-sitting, listening to the playback of the rehearsal on my old Aiwa cassette recorder. I didn't hear the lapses or misses I usually hear when I listen to new songs I've written, then performed as sketches or demos. It was *good*—even I could hear that. I was too excited to sleep that night, but I didn't care. It was in moments like that, sitting in a bathtub listening to a song play back, that I was realizing how, with time and steady practice, I really could swim next to Moby Dick without him eating me. Or me harpooning him. Along with learning what I wanted to get away from, I was figuring out what I wanted to move toward. I knew I wanted to do it harpoonless and with a curious heart.

Chapter 20

Enter the Glamour of a Life in Music

Let's crack open the stinky duck egg of rock and roll mythology, shall we? Our time frame is the very early 2000s. Our location, some lovable, semi-comfortably dog-eared (grimy) rock club in the Midwest at 10:36 p.m. (CT). You and your bandmates have been driving yourselves around the United States on tour in an overpacked van, and you are stretched very, very thin. You are deeply, passionately in love with playing music. Picture yourself standing on a filthy stage facing an audience of about twenty-two people spread out all over the long room, mostly near the bar, which is framed by Christmas lights. The members of this "audience" are nowhere near you; they keep their distance like feral cats. They are there to drink, which is the first order of business; you are a distant second or irritating third. Your goal is to shift that dynamic with your fucking brilliance and undeniable talent. You want to do this not just for attention, but because you feel something for them, even if you aren't sure what that is yet. You don't drive for seven hours in a cramped van if you have zero anticipation of *some* kind of positive interaction. Or at least an interaction? Or just a reaction? For you to even smash this nucleus of a "feeling" into the form of a question will take *years*. Long, tall, pigeon-shit-frosted, painful, joyous years. You don't have any idea what you are trying to show or hold or prove to them, so how do you find out? Especially when you don't even know you are *trying* to find out? You yell your feelings at strangers through a stinky microphone because you don't have the upbringing to know you shouldn't, obviously!

To better paint the scene, we have to back up to about 5:12 p.m. that same day: sound check. You feel hopeful yet slightly irritated. You haven't really gotten enough sleep, your hip hurts from driving, and when you finally pull up to the back of the weedy club load-in area your stomach feels horrible from gas station food you've wanted to fart out like an inflated puffer fish for *hours*! Now you have to carry your heavy, ungainly amp up three flights of warped metal stairs with no banister. None of this is exaggerated. As a person who is prone to exaggeration for entertainment's sake, I'd fully admit if it was.

Here we are at the stage. Daylight is not kind. The stage itself looks constructed from alley detritus, like someone found a reeking, legless billiards table next to a dumpster and decided to drag it in. (I imagine a crane smashing it through the brick wall and letting it land wherever and callin' it good.) We dutifully attach our noisemaking barnacles to it for the night. Now, how about some electricity? There aren't enough outlets for the four capable, scruffy amplifiers our band has brought, let alone grounded ones. Our guitar amplifiers are handsome and ruggedly useful, like Viggo Mortensen in *Lord of the Rings*. Together, the band and the lone soundman (yes, always man. I wish this wasn't such a cliché, but before around 2006 this was a universal truth) dangerously piggyback some extension cords together, creating a loud, standing buzz that will—along with some phantom radio station interference—just have to be our fifth Beatle for this show. C'est la vie. We have our stage positions set and we are kinda plugged in and there are mics on the drums. Now the drummer will hit the drums without ceasing for the next forty-five minutes, sometimes in time with you, but mostly just to hit them. (I am fully guilty of doing this myself every single time I have been given the opportunity.)

Now let's get the vocals up. Woe be to you, O singers. To compete with the alcohol consumption of your target audience, your most important weapon will be the amplified public address system, "PA" for short. I shudder to think what it used to be like before this miracle of technology was developed—folking your ass off until you popped a vein in your neck. The kind of drugs required to get people to pay attention respectfully and focus for that long just aren't fashionable anymore and are also quite illegal. You have to be louder than beer bottles crashing into trash cans and way louder than any frat boys who may be trolling through shrieking their mating call of "BRO!!!!" Time after time you take for granted that the club you are playing that very night will have a sound system that works. It's like the euphoric amnesia I'm told comes over women after they give birth to forget the pain so we will keep breeding despite our ripped and tender under-curtains. You put all the former frustrating, excruciating sound disasters out of your mind and imagine the mysterious, powerful bliss of commanding your voice to soar over the crowd like a dark, sexy eagle, enrapturing everyone and making them fall madly in love with your cruel beauty.

You haven't invested in your own microphone yet because you don't have the money or the time or both. Rock and roll makes doing things during business hours hard enough, and procuring a mic during the day puts you at risk of being late for sound check, which would be rude, and you already had to drive seven hours. That and you're broke as fuck. Fortunately, the club will usually provide the trusty Shure SM58 at no additional charge that you know of yet. *Un*fortunately, it smells like a fish's asshole. Put your mouth and nose up to its gray, mashed little metal grille and breathe in deep with both holes. The smell is so forceful you can pretty much taste it.

"Check, check…uhhh…"

Your voice sounds like it's being piped through a thrift-store whale's carcass into a pirate's wet diaper. *Ahoy, bitch!* You ask the soundman to add some reverb effect into your personal monitor speaker to make this more palatable for the duration. Nine times out of ten he will balk at this suggestion because it would require a little effort outside of the "set it and forget it" empire he rules. During this time of the early 2000s, the soundman is keenly aware that you have an earless vagina and are therefore ignorant of sound engineering and its many guarded mysteries. He's fully convinced he belongs to a very prestigious (if lazy) brotherhood of sound masons who walk the streets by day, just as you or I might, but possess a very important science. After bracing yourself against his condescending "science" you manage to talk him (or fight him) into getting a rudimentary version of what you actually want and run through most of a song. It turns out you've spent so much time dicking around with the basics that your setup time has run out. You will not get a chance to practice the new song you were working on. Fuck. The wave of fresh, reliable disappointment signals that sound check is over and it's time to scramble off to do a bunch of other odd shit before showtime. First, to wash off the condescending science.

You fumble around and find a filthy club bathroom. It's an aromatic closet of cock drawings, industrial fluorescent-pink granular soap, and strangers' pubes. You "clean off" the toilet and sit down with your bag on your lap. You dare not put it down on the sticky, cigarette-butt-covered floor. Written in Sharpie, right at eyeline above the empty toilet paper holder, is the welcome: "Your mom swims out to meet troop ships." You fish around for an industrial brown paper towel and gently scrape your most tender bits. You laugh HARD.

You laugh because there's nothing else you *can* do other than cry about it. And that rarely happens because you are used to it by now.

Then somehow, around 10:36 p.m. (CT), you take all that feeling back up onto the stage. You stand there pretending that you feel worthy enough to be louder than anyone in the room. You play and you sing.

This description of "most rock show beginnings" is the buzzing-fluorescent-tube-lit version, but it is in no way a complaint or written without great affection. The image of the "music business" and of celebrity that we're smashed over the head with looks nothing like the one I inhabit. It's all jets and fleets of limos, soaring moments onstage with dry ice smoking behind you, or soaking in the hot tub of a bedazzled tour bus as a photographer snaps your picture for a magazine spread. But the reality usually involves far more lugging around of amps. There are moments so lonely they become like personal national parks—afterward, you'll never forget the exact place you were standing or the taste left in your mouth. You regain consciousness and walk away an entirely new being. It's both harder than the myth and also contains a more terrible, crunchy joy.

Most of the people making a living as touring musicians work really hard and barely keep it together. We are a lower blue-collar class. Glamour is rare, and when you do find yourself in a nice hotel, you stay all of three hours before you have to go. Don't get me wrong, the ability to get by is gold, but it's a Band-Aid way to live. Nothing is guaranteed and there is no retirement plan or safety net or insurance unless you have a trust fund, and you never come off the road. The next upcoming tour is always like some fetid, rotting rope bridge to an ancient temple. Somebody is gonna get hurt, but there may be glory and treasure, and no matter what, you will get to see old friends and have some exquisite, crippling belly laughs and, hopefully, some transcendent musical moments. And you might just break even.

There is a "thing" that happens on the first show day back after a long spell, which is a very distinct anxiety. It takes hold in the deadly fifteen to thirty minutes before sound check, and then again right before showtime. Those are the moments much of the bulk of rock and roll mythology is based on. Those are the moments when you can't leave; it's *happening*, already in motion. You cannot possibly belong to you.

Those two pockets of time are like the Bermuda Triangle. Many people have been lost there. They are boring *and* terrifying in their way; they are holes that scream for you to shut them up. Addictions are formed there. People fall off the wagon there. People can lose all their self-confidence there. Mental illness is triggered there. Benders are launched from there. Me, I spiral and recall all my anxiety dreams, the ones where I am onstage and the audience starts to leave in disgust as I fumble trying to remember the words of songs *I* wrote. They don't *seem* like dreams at all but real experience. *This night, I will be found out as a fraud, no question. I must already be one, I'm just some jumped-up woman after all...*Those moments make you try to sum up your whole personhood as one static action figure, and it's impossible, but you can't stop *trying* to do it, to force the peg into the hole. You are locked in. It's madness. Like I said, and it can't be understated: Many people have been lost there. It's as if the poison fountain that has given you all the power you have to fake your way to this moment wants it all back *now*! And with interest. It will turn all your thoughts and bodily liquids into strychnine. It's kinda like the bad twentieth-century American myth of "The Crossroads," *if* I believed in something as stupid as "The Devil," and if there was soul-eating involved. But it's too late now, you are at the mic, and fraud or not, you have to make a believable noise or die trying.

Chapter 21

What Lives on the Road

"The music business" may be a hungry, exhausting bore, but it's one in which you can meet some truly dedicated and amazing people. They even outnumber the scoundrels most of the time. You'll never know enough to "get ahead." You will never know the "formula" to making it "big." There may have been something to it a long time ago, but not anymore. "Formulas" are made by people who already have a ton of money. Nowadays, streaming makes sure those who write the songs and perform them will get nothing. They mold the willing ("I want to be famous!") and the unwilling ("I'm only ten years old!") into shapes and make them make the sounds and do the dances and the press photos and interviews and, and, and…A few outliers spring their way into the big time, lovely unicorns each of them out there in the long green grass, but the gatekeepers are stacked *deep*. Most of us will be greeted with a "You shall not pass!" (albeit never said with that much directness). You've heard this sad tale before, and you already don't care, so...I'll stop. But if you just want to make music for music's sake it can be an incredibly rewarding business to be in.

Along the way, I had to learn the ropes from scratch. I can't say I had many pleasant surprises about the industry itself. The first tour I ever went on was playing drums for a band called Cub. This was during my first years as a musician, when I was still living in Tacoma. Cub was from Vancouver, and I had recorded a couple songs with them in Olympia. Their drummer could not go out of town as she was the manager of a chocolate factory (the best, most fairy-tale reason ever!). We were opening for the Smugglers, from Vancouver, BC, and Seaweed, who I knew from Tacoma. We were all friends. It was Robynn (who would later become my roommate in Vancouver), Lisa, Bill, and me in Lisa's parents' car, a green sedan with just enough room to sleep upright. The Canadian drives were *so* long I got used to marathon travel early on. We sometimes drove *eight* hours before we had to play a show. We were in our twenties, so it just wasn't a big deal. That first tour branded me a touring musician forever, and I'm forever grateful to Cub for taking me on that imagination-exploding mission. We were out for a month and a week. We went everywhere.

Cub took me on my second huge tour as well, in 1995, during the same period I was playing with Maow. We went out on the road supporting the Muffs, a dream realization so giant I had a hard time even fathoming it. At our first show at Bottom of the Hill in San Francisco, we were greeted warmly by the other support band we shared the bill with, the Queers. This was the first night of a six-week tour. I was so heavy into the

Muffs, I could barely say hello when I first met Kim Shattuck. She fronted the band on vocals and guitar, and there is no other way to say it, she was my idol. The Muffs were right up there with the Flat Duo Jets for me. Kim was a monster, and I had loved her since she was in the Pandoras with Melanie Vammen (who had also been in the Muffs). Kim was SO tough. She was about six feet tall and made guitars howl. She could scream like a mountain lion, and she was who I wanted to be. And if that wasn't enough, my favorite rock and roll drummer, Roy McDonald, from Redd Kross, was also in the band. Rounding out the three was fantastic bass player Ronnie Barnett. He was the warmest, funniest, most welcoming person.

All three bands on that tour became lifelong friends. The chemistry was electric. We did it all: drinking, fighting, throwing a malfunctioning TV off a balcony (Kim's work). We ate cheap road food, got lost, narrowly escaped possible serial killer basements offered as lodgings. Got bad haircuts, vintage clothes, and running hangovers. We raged from coast to coast. The final coup de grâce was when I fixed our rental van in front of a mechanic who didn't "feel like it" in Idaho. I wasn't fucking having it. I was over men holding my fate in the balance so casually. I used duct tape and Form-A-Gasket and we were off, birds flipped full mast. Losing Kim to ALS in the fall of 2019 was one of the major blows in my life. We were not super close, but we were always happy to see each other. She was so alive, with a beastly energy I could taste when I met her. She had a force of something too big to contain in her body, a quality she shared with Dexter Romweber of the Flat Duo Jets. She was my hero who lived it and proved it right in front of me, welcoming me along. Watching her, I silently made a glittery little mental note that I was not alone in my muchness. I miss her but I still feel her; I still have that glittery little note tucked into my heart sleeve.

The year I recorded *The Virginian*, I also began playing with the New Pornographers, a band Carl Newman had started around the same time he was helping with guitar on the album. Back then, the band was comprised of Carl, Dan Bejar, Blaine Thurier, Fisher Rose, and John Collins. I was so in awe of Carl and Dan as songwriters that I couldn't believe Carl asked me to be a singer in the band. At the same time, I was self-managing my own music, continuing to play in Maow, and doing a lot of booking while still going to art school. All of the labeling and shipping and dubbing and legwork and band practice hadn't lost its shine. When I got dumped and the major-record-label deal came to naught, I was lucky to have this roster of activities and busywork to cling to.

My first solo tour was across Canada, and it was during this time I met the musician Dallas Good, who would become a lifelong friend and collaborator. Dallas came out to Vancouver sight unseen, recommended by the great Brian Connelly to play guitar on the tour. He was a really tall, thin man with dark hair, a little younger than me, and a kid-like sunshine smile that would light his face. We hit it off immediately. We were giggling idiots. We talked *constantly* about music. Dallas was from Toronto, and he was the real deal. Along with his brother Travis and their band, the Sadies, I hadn't met any other musicians with such a similar aesthetic to mine as to what the sounds should be. They were ferocious guitar players, worked hard, and were effortlessly cool. For my next record, *Furnace Room Lullaby*, I lost no time asking the Sadies to be the band for the second half of the tour. They had played all over the record anyway.

I was now ready to book my first North American tour. I was overextended and still in dumpsville, so the energies didn't exactly align—my excitement about the tour became a kind of punch-drunk madness. First of all, I would not accept that it's a bad idea to play Seattle and Phoenix on back-to-back dates. It's a TWENTY-ONE HOUR DRIVE! I couldn't bear to say no to a show, though, and just figured, *We'll drive overnight! No big deal!* I had road lust *bad*. It was the decision-making of a greedy, delusional nut. The Seattle gig started a downward spiral that I took the Sadies along for. It was a rough show. I had found out that my ex Chauncey's new wife had been at the show the night before in Vancouver, BC, and I had a bit of an explosion onstage at the Tractor in Ballard: "Don't come to my work, bitch! What's *wrong* with you!? Do you want my *whole* fucking life!?" I was ablaze, a bleeding sack of hurt and an alienating force all at once. It was in this state—tired and streaked with tears—that I headed to Phoenix with my sweet friends, the Sadies, to play the show I'd booked for us the next day.

Now, the Sadies are not ones to shrink from a challenge, they are *brutal* road dogs, but as hour after hour on the highway went by, one truth became evident: *twenty-one hours in a go is too much.* We arrived and played the Phoenix show, having hustled all that way to play to pretty much an empty room.

That night, probably because he was tired, Dallas broke his ankle playing a game of basketball at the house where we were staying. Hearing him yelling, I did the kind thing you do when a friend badly injures himself and went out and shouted at him for waking me up. (It was a bizarre reaction; I was just exhausted and not fully taking things in. And I think it was a trigger from all those years of waking up to drunk people yelling.) We got into a big fight that hung in the air for days after. Dallas was twenty-six then, a couple of years younger than me, and as he walked along with his cane, he would glare at me (rightfully) like a bad guy in a horror movie. I got the stink eye for a while.

The sour feelings of the tour ebbed and Dallas and I made up, but there was a lingering bad taste. The tour hadn't made money, and then I had to come up with a thousand bucks to cover the damage when I dinged the rental van. Not being in a great communication mode, I failed to explain that to the Sadies, which led them to believe I had just kept all the money from the tour. A fair amount of time later, we talked about all the misunderstandings and I sorry'd my ass off. I felt *terrible* I'd let so much time go by without talking to them about everything that had happened. It was 1999, the new century just around the corner. I was twenty-nine, a few years into performing solo and so tired and out of sorts from scrambling to move myself forward. I had been my least considerate self and am so lucky that my friends forgave me. Even Dallas and I made up, to the point that now, remembering him lasering hostile looks in my direction is a weirdly sweet, even funny memory. Dallas, sitting next to me in the van, both hands crossed over his cane like a praying mantis, glaring at me like Vincent Price.

A couple of years later, when I was living in Tucson and finally sort of had my shit together, I decided that I wanted to make a live record, because no one ever *did*! I had been researching and found out most well-known "live" records were faked with overdubs and canned crowd sounds. I was aghast.

Well, *I'm* gonna make a real one, I raged to myself. There was no question who I was going to ask to be the band; it was the Sadies hands down. I missed them terribly *and* I had a real booking agent at this point. The idea was we would write original songs together, play songs from our catalogs, along with any covers that meant a lot to us. No one was writing original songs to be released for the first time on a *live* recording at that time—that was incredibly rare even twenty years prior—which made the project seem like a dare and therefore even more fun. We recruited Jon Rauhouse, Kelly Hogan, Carolyn Mark, and Jim & Jennie and the Pinetops to form our tour armada when the songs were written and it was time to hit the road.

We played several nights at Schubas in Chicago, Lee's Palace in Toronto, and finally Toronto's incredible country music institution, the Matador. We had the *best* time, and I was so glad to be back with my music soul mates again. The funny part was I thought mixing a live record would be a breeze compared to a studio record, as you'd have fewer tracks to choose from. Nope. I was dead wrong, as I always am about these things. I thought I'd know how to do it by now—having made three albums—but every record is different, and the truth was I had only sharpened my ability to hear mistakes, potential trouble, or what I hadn't yet captured, its absence registering in my body as a baffling gnaw: *Did I pick the right tunnel down the rabbit hole?* I also have acute high-end hearing, so things bother me that other people can't hear. For example, I can hear electricity. Most people can't. I had no idea, I just thought everybody could. It made me a little nuts trying to describe certain kinds of distortion I wanted to notch out. There would always be some new challenge in recording, and I decided I needed to just roll with it. I had to concede it was the mighty rabbit hole of possibility that would always be in control of my record making. I had to accept it and go in like a newborn baby every time from then on. It didn't mean I shouldn't respect my experience or ability, it just meant I had to be open to the human capacity to take things in and see further than before. The tools get sharper, and the horizon gets farther away. It's a beautiful human conundrum to be in.

Being in many bands at once has kept me on the road for most of my life now. I would travel with one band, then another, then miss the band I was not with. I remember being on tour in Halifax and feeling homesick for everyone all at once. I wanted all the friends I played music with to come and enjoy this great time with me! I used a brown pay phone on the street corner to call Dan Bejar just to leave him a voice mail about how great his new record (Destroyer's *City of Daughters*) was. That pay phone triggered some emotional tidal wave and I wrote "Calling Cards" for *all* my bandmates. I didn't write love songs for or about boyfriends (that shit was *dumb*), but I did write them about my band family.

For all the bad things that can happen on tour, there are ten times the number of good things. Late-night drives spawn the greatest laughter, camaraderie, and inspiration. I've seen wildlife in ways people don't usually get to, like a moose in rut attacking our van near Schreiber, Ontario, as we flew past at seventy-five miles per hour. I'll never forget the blurred white of its very angry, very horny eye! We were so lucky not to collide. Drifts of delicate-looking pronghorns, Oklahoma scissor-tailed flycatchers, giant Montana porcupines, bears of every kind. Herds of elk stopping us in the road. Wolves in Montana and on the Apache reservation in Arizona. Coatis in New Mexico, bats in Texas. Endless white-tailed and mule deer across the continent. So many special creatures and plants and weather systems.

Many things defy description. Flipped semis balancing upside down on the concrete median that contradict the laws of physics; peach and watermelon sunsets you can taste; a rabid, golden Saint Bernard rushing our speeding van outside Paducah, Kentucky, which broke my heart; hate-speech billboards put up by Christians in Missouri; loving affirmational graffiti for strangers by strangers in *every* city; pelicans suddenly rising like a swarm of army choppers over a sea cliff in Santa Cruz. A stacked tower of televisions in an open field in Idaho, blending in by reflecting the gold grass on their convex glass monitor screens; humans doing kind deeds by the thousands. A lone man on a scruffy pinto quarter horse riding down Central Avenue in Albuquerque at 5:00 a.m.—he even stopped for the light. Friendly lizards who sit with you for a cup of coffee. Far too many police lights. Pristine mountain peaks you can't take in completely with your puny little human eyes; a shark recoiling up over my foot on the beach in San Diego; getting hailed offstage by literal hail. So many variations of northern lights: a flickering wall of rainbow fire above the Canadian Rockies; a ruby-red mushroom over southern Idaho; a neon-white band of ribbon over the Manitoba prairies that wavered, shimmered, then ripped itself apart. The most unholy filthy toilets known to mankind. Sprawling, galling, reckless development and destruction. Signs telling me to reverse my vasectomy. Massive, bearded trees and acres of migrating endangered cranes out in stubbly fields and wetlands. Buildings and landscape destroyed by disasters. Buildings thought too far gone, then brought back by caring communities, like the Howard Theatre in DC. The post-9/11 aftermath in NYC and its kind citizens *still* coming to see us play and making *us* feel good. A blizzard coating the abandoned mansions in Detroit, a Technicolor pheasant stepping out of one of the doorways, so gorgeous and bizarre we were all glad we hadn't seen it alone. The topmost turrets and windows in the most beautiful theaters from other centuries. Cities in their latest possible nighttime clothes, glittering and cold and quiet looking, just a little bit gentle. The baton handoff of the night and morning shifts, a family of ducks crossing *both* east- and westbound sections of I-94 outside Detroit and *none* of them getting hit. Golden hour in every state and province in North America. Fruit in shapes and flavors I never knew existed in New Zealand. What a staggeringly beautiful world.

Chapter 22

Things Your Parents Won't Tell You

The whole time I was moving and traveling around those years of my early thirties, my dad was declining. When I'd call up, his voice sounded a million miles away. The dad he'd been the day we went shopping for a van had receded, and I wouldn't see that form of him again. He never found a job after getting fired from the last one, and he was often drunk, always sad, and increasingly paranoid. He was living in a basement studio apartment in Seattle that his sister Nancy had found for him. He wouldn't accept any help. Not from his family and not from the government, except for an occasional secret doctor visit to the VA for help with his back pain and alcoholism. At some point, not long after I'd moved to Tucson and four years into the new century, he just gave up. He would call me out of nowhere extremely agitated, raving about Osama bin Laden, claiming he was being tracked by government authorities because he "knew too much," having seen something he shouldn't have while on guard duty at Fort Belvoir when I was a baby. He was obsessed, ranting. On these calls, he terrified me, the same way the old Seventh-Day Adventist reel-to-reel tapes had when they'd be booming through our house in Vancouver. He was *so* afraid of being tracked down and killed, my heart broke for him.

"I saw too much," he'd say, and he'd be crying.

It was during this time that I wrote the song "I Wish I Was the Moon." The sadness of my dad's situation was on my mind a lot, and the song, written on scraps of paper, came out fairly quickly. I finished it with Jon Rauhouse, guitar wunderkind, in the living room of his house in Phoenix. We worked over his low coffee table and played guitars together. Sitting there, making that song with Jon, was solace in the hopelessness of this time—an act of creation as my dad seemed dedicated more and more every month to extinguishing himself.

My aunt Nancy and I tried to get him into rehab, but he refused to go. He was a religious person so thought suicide was a sin, but I guess he figured he could fool Jesus if he drank himself to death, which he did. He had a massive heart attack and was found naked and dead in his basement room.

When I got the news I felt no surprise. My dad had given us the cruel assignment of watching him die. Of putting us in the position of seeing him walk toward death as we shouted and waved our hands and tried to grab at his arms to save him.

When I was a kid, he'd always been unknowable to me. But there were brief moments where I could see something in him that was kindred, like when he'd gently pet Buffy or look transported by music. But mostly he'd seemed shy and disengaged. I had hated, too, how he'd allowed his sister Carol and her terrible husband Junior to rule over our house with their wrathful and punishing God—and their devil, who was always lurking on the rainy street outside.

It wasn't so long after his death that my aunt Nancy told me something that helped the puzzle pieces of my dad fall into place. She said that when he'd been a kid, he and Carol had been molested together by a supposed "friend of the family." I was disgusted and surprised. But the surprise only lasted for a short while. The more I thought about it, it really added up. He was a strange man. Not that being abused *makes* you strange, he just had some very peculiar ways of parenting that I'm sure were a direct result of his horrifying experience. He only got me a babysitter once. She was OK, but her little brother trapped me in their A-frame doghouse and threw dirt clods at me, in that terrifying *Lord of the Flies* way one kid will sometimes hunt down another. As soon as he heard about it, my dad said, "You're never going back there." After that, I never had an adult watch me who wasn't related to us, and even that was rare. He must have decided it was safer for me to be alone and unsupervised. It also explained the incident with the school counselor after my mom "died," why he had acted so quickly and vehemently, in a way so out of character, yelling at the teacher and gravely forbidding me to go into an office alone with anyone.

I could now understand other pieces of him, too, like the symbiotic dependency he had with Carol, and why Junior's devil would have made a terrible kind of sense to him—something evil standing right outside your house, just waiting to snatch you up. He'd been trapped there, in childhood, and never fully escaped. As he'd declined at the end of his life, all those old fears and injuries had returned in full force. I thought back to those raving phone calls, where he'd talk about "knowing too much," and I understood what it was he hadn't been able to tell me.

Rape and abuse perpetuate trauma long after they occur. Trauma is a disease that just keeps traumatizing and re-traumatizing everyone around the initial victim. After Nancy told me this piece of his history, I could no longer hold it against my dad that he wanted to go, that he had never really been present in the first place. I could only burn with the idea of someone destroying whole families with their evil deeds. Deeds that sacrifice little children and then make them walk through an entire life hating themselves for it. My poor father.

My mom reappears at this newly vulnerable time in my life. Fleeting through like a deer. Of course she does. After my aunt Nancy's disclosure, I found myself returning to the different memories I had of being a kid, sifting around in them to see if I could turn up new colors. I'd picked up early that what my parents had in common, besides being poor as shit, was that they'd both been too young to become parents. Now I knew this other thing they had in common, which was that they'd both been the victims of terrible abuse in their childhoods. And I was their child who had been raped when I wasn't yet fifteen. I would remember my father lifting me on his shoulders, taking me through a field filled with deer. Or my mom staring with cold eyes at me as I stood at the sink with a bandanna on my head, saying, "You're going to become vain." The puppy I'd name Buffy making her way up the stairs of the tiny house where we lived, a wriggling gift because my mom was about to leave. All the memories had a different cast to them now.

Both times, I learned about my parents' abuse sideways. In my dad's case from my aunt; and in my mom's, in that diner ride with my stepdad Bill. Looking back at my childhood, I slowly understood that even if no one talked about it, these secrets had been a distress signal that buzzed all through it, a frequency that's too low to hear, but you can still feel pulsing through the air, shaping you—with its invisible currents and dial tones—into the person you become.

In a way I knew nothing about my parents.

And in another way I did. When I think back to my early kid love for fairy tales and folktales, I see how I was drawn to them not just as entertainments, but as a practical, everyday guidebook for life. This is, after all, how such stories have worked for eons, containing useful information like "don't get eaten by wild animals," "depression is probably going to haunt you," "mushrooms are tricky," and so on. They warn you of how a wolf might one day come to your house and speak to you with your mother's own sweet voice.

Even today, I still love how these old stories and songs give great respect to animals and nature. And how through them we have fleeting access to the ancient deities of the Slavic peoples, gods who, with all their infinite combinations of craft and ability and gender/non-gender, came and went and made the earth work and the grass grow and elements sentient. Sometimes you can even detect a trace of the women; it's been a long time since Christianity sunk its teeth in and shook hard, trying to break the necks of our spirits. So much of the feminine has been washed away, but the old witch Baba Yaga is still in there.

A large swath of Slavic tales feature what's called a psychopomp, an animal or a trickster god who acts as a guide to the protagonist in the story. A sort of left-field Greek chorus. As a teen, I had only the thinnest understanding of what "psychopomp" meant when I first heard the word, but I knew *immediately* that I wanted to be one. In the old tales, the psychopomp doles out the clues—cryptic but always correct—that allow the protagonist to solve an important riddle or find the path out of the forest themselves. Like a psychopomp, I wanted to inhabit a den in the forest and possess the answers to transformation and growth that I'd croak out now and then to visitors. That sounded like a dream come true. I still remember the day someone I trusted told me that humans can't be psychopomps. I was crushed. I didn't have a library or internet at the ready so I just sat in that sad little diaper of truth longer than I should have...thirty-some years? When I finally looked it up, it turned out the working description of "psychopomp" I'd had was less incorrect than "incomplete." If I had understood psychopomps to be animals that help you solve a problem or find a path, other sources describe them as "conductors of souls" to the afterlife. Among many other ways of being, as it turns out, psychopomps can perform all sorts of other tasks and roles too, including being singers.

But there I was with nothing but that foggy half-knowledge and a deep desire to be one. I liked these stories. Liked their forests, their animals. Their teeth. I knew that translation from their original Slavic languages had likely changed them, and so back in my twenties, when Tacoma Community College began offering night classes in the Russian language, I'd signed up.

I was twenty then. I made it a year and a half before I transferred to art school in Canada, which, unsurprisingly, did *not* offer Russian courses. I'm a greedy learner and an overreacher, so I thought I'd never stop learning the language, I'd just "come back to it later," which I didn't. It breaks my heart, really. Russian is difficult. A year and a half barely gets you conjugating a verb and learning genitive case, so reading the stories of my Slavic ancestors *myself* to look for their meanings and poetry didn't happen. Still, the stories have stayed with me. If the story of the sad man who accidentally rescues sorrow from a hole in the ground can make me weep like a child even when it's been translated into English, I can only imagine what it'd be like to read it in the singsongy rhythm of the Ukrainian.

I was hunting something in these stories. I know it has to be more than a love of dark fairy tales that has kept me following this trail of inquiry over the years, more than just having a skewed, irreverent sense of doom and humor. It runs deeper, like a kind of psychic loneliness. With my family unwilling to say out loud the truths about who we were, I instinctively knew these tales contained some important pieces of family history.

And then, in my thirties, I ended up moving from the tales to real life. I wanted to know how our family had ended up in Whatcom County, Washington. What had we been running from or to? I went to visit a great-uncle, Bill, the brother of my maternal grandfather. He had some old family photos and documents that he said I could photocopy.

One item was our family's immigration document. It was in Russian. I asked Bill if he knew what it said.

"No, I only speak fake Russian. We are Ukrainian, and I can't read the writing anyway."

He had come to America too young to have had any schooling in Russia, so he had never learned to read Cyrillic. But *I* could, thanks to that year and a half at Tacoma Community College. Sure, I couldn't understand what the words meant, but I *could* speak them out loud. I could read *our* fairy tale! Phonetically, at least. So I read the paperwork to Bill and he translated.

The document was later lost in a house fire, but here's what I remember: The ship my great-grandparents traveled to America on had left from Germany, and before that they had lived in Saratov, Russia, an industrial city on the Volga, northeast of Ukraine. This was before the Russian Revolution. I don't know why they came to the United States. I suppose I didn't ask. I was too caught up in amazement. It's crazy how easy it is to go to great lengths to find out about something important only to go home having forgotten the point of your whole trip until it's too late. But I had the documents, and I didn't think I'd ever lose them. And I also didn't think about the fact that my uncle would someday die.

I was surprised to learn we were Ukrainian when I had thought we were Russian, but not shocked. Not exactly. Our family name was Shevchenko, and a couple of friends as well as my Russian teacher had pointed out that it wasn't a Russian name. Russians are very patriarchal, and your name should end with an *a* if you are a female. The *o* at the end of

"Shevchenko" is neutral and ungendered, which is Ukrainian. What strikes me about the incident is how it took only one generation—one!—to erase my family's ethnic origins, stories, experiences, and language.

And there's a parallel to how other family stories and histories disappeared, so that you, the kid coming after the erasure, don't know how to make sense of the bizarre behaviors of the adults around you: "Why are they so angry?" "Why do they hate each other?" "Why can't they just *stop* drinking?" "Why do they hit me for nothing?"

As a kid, it seemed so obvious that there was a violent force breathing hard behind us, dragging itself, wounded and angry, toward us faster than we could run. Eventually, my parents were destroyed by it. But nobody would tell me its name or where it had come from. No wonder I went looking in all these old folktales trying to find answers. No wonder I wanted to turn myself into a creature who knew all the answers. But I already was. After all, the werewolf in me is from an old country, even if I'm not. You can see it in the fur on my fingers, the catch in my walking gait, my anxious impatience that makes it hard for me to relax.

The only stories I have of my family seem like lies, and when I tell them they sound more like Eastern fairy tales—dark and funny. Feral and without a moral, just disappearance and sadness; bizarre little Technicolor landscapes. The great Eastern sadness whispers to me that it is one of the unbreakable pillars of observation, and that I should cherish and respect it. So I do.

This is the story of my maternal grandfather, Nikolas Shevchenko, known in America as Nick Hobbs...and it is, too, the story of how my mother came to be a deer, always just out of reach.

Once in the country of Russia, in a metal-gray city on the stolid Volga, a pair of twins was born. They were nothing special, just two baby boys. As they grew, they became slightly different, then more and more different. The one named Ivan was outgoing and athletic. He loved to run and play and climb things. He was a boy's boy, but he was also the apple of the eye of his mother, Olga. What a splendid child he was! The other twin, Niko, was more inward. He was interested in music and poetry. He did his schoolwork. He liked to draw and to listen rather than talk. He worked no less hard than his brother, but somehow he managed to draw his mother's scorn. Olga was a dominating woman, disgust her primary way of communicating. Nobody else was going to make sure things got done! It was all on her, and she resented it: "Men just let things die!" In the case of her son, she resented him preemptively, as he hadn't even made up his mind to be a no-account yet! It wasn't fair. But alas, she didn't even know she was doing it. And none dared enlighten her, not that they understood it, either. At some point, while still in Saratov, Ivan, the golden twin, drowned. Niko's remaining presence enraged his mother. "It should have been you!" she would hiss. Niko crumpled inward like a tin can. As he warped, his sharp edges pierced his already shrinking heart.

Olga was irritated by the sensitivity and artistic nature of this son, and resented him as if he'd killed his own brother. Even after they had immigrated to America and he married my grandmother and had a family of his own and a farm, Olga, now "Baba," would call him "faggot" and say he was less than a man. Meanwhile, she adored his children. It must have felt so surreal that she would openly love and accept his children and *still* hate him. So *painful*.

My mother was Baba's favorite. She doted on her. My grandfather bore this through clenched teeth, and began to resent his own daughter. Then he just hated her. She was only fourteen when he raped her in the barn. Her childish upset sent my grandfather over the edge. He was taken by a torrential rage and so turned to destroy her. He did. Utterly.

I don't know if my Gramma Mary Ann ever knew he'd raped their daughter, but she knew he was violent. My grandmother was not one to take things quietly. She would harp on him and he in turn would beat her. It's said my mother once intervened and stabbed him with a kitchen knife for fear he was going to kill my gramma. I don't know if he raped my mother before or after this. The marriage dissolved. Baba and Deid (my great-grandfather Fredric) disappeared from the story. My grandmother divorced my grandpa Nick and later remarried, to the gentle bachelor Clyde.

Sometimes, when she was by herself, she would just rock back and forth and back and forth, like all the other women on that side of my family.

This history makes me feel sorry for my mother, and still I have to keep my heart hard. She's a grifter.

When I say that, I don't mean that she stole money. She never did that. Her confidence trick was to make me think she might love me—might, after all, be glad she had a daughter. I fell for it over and over. I would shape-shift into new permutations, creep around the house trying to be as small and quiet and invisible and helpful as a kid could be—and it still didn't work. I'd still do something wrong, like ask for a space costume. Always, something would make her spring away from me. Move out, drive off, become a blur. And then, when that wasn't enough, she faked her own death, leaving me, at age eight, to mourn her.

As an adult I'd learned there was a word for what my mom did: "pseudocide." Wikipedia informs me that pseudocide "is the act of an individual purposely deceiving other people into believing that the individual is dead, when the person is, in fact, still alive.…People who commit pseudocide can do so by leaving evidence, clues, or through other methods." The entry then lists the reasons that a person might choose to do this, such as to collect insurance money or "arouse false sympathy." The reason that seems most like my mom's is this one: "to evade pursuit." As I'd understood it as a kid, she'd come down with cancer and, overwhelmed by the illness, had gone off, like a deer pursued by death who sprints away to evade it.

If I recognized her actions as cruel when I was a kid, I quashed the thought down and packed it away—I was too over-joyed to have her back. As I got older, I began to comprehend that I seemed to be the only person who had been told the lie—that the funeral party thrown for me to attend had been like a play staged for a single audience member, me. Still, even as I absorbed this, I was becoming old enough to understand that people get confused when they're scared—they make bad decisions, and what would I do if I was young and had cancer? I might do some random thing like run off to Hawaii, too.

There was much I could have forgiven. But it was the grift of her that ground that down—that love held out to dance before me, always snatched back just as I reached out my arms for it. It was our infernal pattern, present when I was a kid, continued when I became an adult. We wouldn't talk for a while, and then there would come a call that she needed me, and I would spring forth, to save the day. Go to where she was to help her move out from the house of some terrible husband or boyfriend, find her a new place to live, or somehow fix whatever awful thing was happening. Through my thirties I was happy to do it, happy to be her mark. As I'd gotten older, I needed my dad less, and we'd been able to work out a kind of makeshift relationship. We could share a meal or watch TV in a silence that didn't feel weighted and sad. I suppose I hoped I could work out something like that with my mom, that maybe we could find some kind of alliance, no matter how jury-rigged and Scotch-taped together. But every time she flashed back in my life, just as I came into range close enough to touch her, she'd flee. And as she left, she'd always make one thing clear: The reason it hadn't worked out was me. Because I asked to leave too early, or too late. Was packing the boxes wrong or asked her to use certain cleaning supplies when washing up in the kitchen. I'd been a pain in the ass in some way. A drag. Been too bossy—or just too much.

That was her grift: to make me want her and then disappear all over again. That's what I can't forgive.

The breaking point happened when I was living in Tucson. I had offered her my house to live in, and she'd moved in but then bailed after I chided her for her terrible-smelling cigarette butts she'd brought in from outside to throw away in the trash. This sort of skipping out had happened before, but this time, the dirt in my mouth tasted different. I was tired of it. Tired of being the mark. I'd just been nominated for a Grammy for my sixth album, *Middle Cyclone*. The whole time we were arranging the new place, my mom never mentioned a *thing* about it. And I hated the part of me that wanted her to, like it was some terrible vanity to be proud of something I'd done and want my parent to say, "Good job, kid." Then she moved out without telling me, leaving me with no renter and no one to care for the house.

I wrote her a long letter. I told her that I didn't want anything to do with her anymore. I told her I didn't blame her for not wanting a child, that I understood about not knowing what to do when you have cancer, that I understood why she panicked and left when I was little. I said I needed to not feel like a little circus dog dancing for her attention anymore. I needed to take the hint; she didn't want a daughter. I sent the letter and never looked back.

Weeks went by. I was sitting in the changing kiosk of a doctor's office. I had already received one piece of good news that day—that I didn't have a cyst on one of my ovaries. And then I received a second: The biopsy on my right breast had come back clean. It wasn't cancer. I was sitting there, feeling tremendous relief, when a truth hit me: *My mother had likely NEVER had cancer.*

It was so obvious! How hard had I worked to keep that lie in circulation my *whole life*. I had lost pieces of my soul doing it. All the times over the past few years I had asked her about her illness, so I'd better understand my own health risks, came flooding back. She'd had a different answer every time, oscillating between cervical, uterine, and ovarian. Sitting bare assed on the changing bench, the realization was like urine soaking a pair of pants, warm and creeping. I felt my skin crawl. I knew why I had never allowed myself to understand this before. If my mom didn't have cancer, it would have meant she left all those years ago because she didn't want *me*. The pursuit she was evading wasn't death, it was me—second-grade me. I looked down at the underwear in my hand, trying to remember what I was doing. How could I have been so willfully stupid? I guess I was staving off the inevitable until I could handle it, at this perfect moment in time, when I had already cut her out of my life, sitting naked as a wet cat in a gynecologist's changing room, behind a flimsy flowered curtain.

Finally realizing the full extent of my mother's deception felt partly like awe and partly like looking at the empty, scorched spot left where the fortune teller's trailer had sat just the night before. She was gone with the carnival on whatever invisible, sinister road they travel. It was almost like she had never been there at all, but there was wreckage in her wake: my missing childhood, my lack of ability to trust and be loved, my sense of not belonging. And it wasn't even a surprise. After all, hadn't I known this was coming since I first began dreaming as a kid?

I wish it was easy to be done with people just because you want to be. To write them a letter and never think about them again. Even now, she still haunts my dreams, always there and then gone. I do not know her. She is a blur of auburn, of hoof, of shivering teeth. She killed herself when I was a kid, and there is nothing I'd like to do more than to kill her, too. To be done. To have nothing to remember her by but a tall, awkward marker of stones in a field somewhere, picked by her when she was a kid, before I knew her. But I cannot kill her—not because I'm too good a person, but because even now I don't know her well enough to choose the right weapon.

Chapter 23

Happier Inheritances and Returns

In 2004, my friend Ruth Leitman asked me to contribute some music to her documentary *Lipstick and Dynamite: The First Ladies of Wrestling*, about the first US female wrestlers of the 1950s. This group of women became infamous, and their celebrity cost them a great deal—as soon as I heard about the project, of course I wanted to be a part of it. About five minutes into watching a screener of the film, I learned that one of the wrestlers, Ella Waldek, was actually named Elsie Shevchenko.

Wait, that was my mom's family's name before it became Hobbs.

Waldek, the narration continued, had been from Custer, Washington.

Could we be…?

I paused the movie and frantically dialed my Gramma Mary Ann.

"Oh, yeeeessss…she was quite famous," she said casually.

You will recognize by now that this is my grandmother's trade-mark move. It was the same way she'd revealed that she used to sing in a country harmony band. That side of my family—a more tight-lipped group of clams you'll never meet. I knew this about them, and still I was thunderstruck. *How could no one have EVER mentioned her?* I was THIRTY-FOUR at the time, for god's sake! How had this famous wrestling great-aunt NEVER come up in conversation?

Ella had grown up on a farm in Washington, then made her way to Chicago, where she competed in roller derby before finding her way to wrestling. One of her stage names was "Charming Carmen." Tragically, a woman she fought in the ring, Janet Wolfe, died after a match. Ella was cleared of any wrongdoing, but for a long time after people would chant "murderer" as she went to fight.

It was so much to take in—I could see echoes all across her story of something familiar in me. Ella, too, had made it out, and by the time I met her, she was in her mid-seventies. She was living in Florida but came to Toronto for the film's pre-miere. I was in town playing with the Corn Sisters, at the event for the film held at the Horseshoe Tavern. Ruth introduced us. Back in her younger days, Ella had looked like a Soviet pro-paganda sculpture: a thick, well-muscled body in fierce for-ward motion. Now she had shortish, blond-gray hair and was dressed in a plain sweater and slacks, wearing only a little jew-elry. She looked not unlike my uncle Bill, her cousin and my grandfather's brother. They both had slightly thick, potato-y features, not at all unattractive, just stronger than average, like how draft horses look when compared to riding horses. She was absolutely singular, her granite presence setting her apart from a stereotypical old white lady. She was like no one I'd met before or since, even when making polite small talk in her gravelly sailor's voice.

She eyed me a little sidelong as we shook hands. I introduced myself, explaining how we were related. She relaxed a bit then, but I could see right away that although she didn't exude it in an offensive way, Ella wasn't someone who invited intimacy. Like the rest of my family, she didn't give anything away. Still, at the end of the night we exchanged addresses and agreed to keep in touch. In the end, who she became to me was Elsie Mecouch, my aunt who lived in Florida, not Ella Waldek, famous wrestling star. Neither of us were going to look back to our biological Ukrainian families for connection—we knew it was a dry well or worse. Years later, in 2013, she passed away from cancer. She had already had it awhile by the time we met. She told me it was painless and just biding its time. She wasn't afraid of it—and that seemed of a piece with who she was.

She remains with me in an odd way—an embodiment of another kind of inheritance from the family. The will to fight, to punch out with your arm, to use your teeth if you have to, but to never roll over and let life happen to you.

There were other gifts like this over the years, moments when the past returned, but this time brought with it something sweeter.

Over time, my recurring dream of my mom was replaced

with other dreams, ones where someone who had gone was returned to me.

There were three of these in all. Just like in a fairy tale.

The first: I was back in Vancouver, BC, at Miller Block Studio to work on my second album, *Furnace Room Lullaby*, with Darryl Neudorf. I slept in an old office room down a long hallway of gray, spongy carpet. There were six or seven of these rooms, mostly uninhabited and mainly used for storage. There were no windows. The studio was on the second floor above a used-CD and pawn shop, the building barricaded with wood and welded metal fencing against the marauding junkies outside. Hastings Street was a drug hot spot where horrible fates played out. A lot of the people there were just trying to get by, but the drugs made it an unpredictable, often dangerous scene. Quiet could explode into something devastating in seconds. Alone in my office room, it sometimes felt like I was existing in the science fiction movie *Escape from New York*, all of humanity turned up to screaming decibels. The epidemic of Indigenous women going missing was at one of its terrible heights, and fear permeated the neighborhood as the powers that be ignored what was happening. It was the Green River Killer all over again.

I slept on a couch with a pile of CDs I'd gotten from the "courting" record company near my head. I clung to them. I listened to Mark Lanegan and Cat Power and held on for dear life. I was adrift, though the recording process kept a faint, wispy tether on my ankle. Everything was charged and uncomfortable.

One night in the deep, still dark, I dreamt of my friend Rick, the one from Tacoma who had been killed when a tree fell on his car. He was calling, and I picked up the phone with great excitement. I was in a large brass bed from the eighteen hundreds with lots of colorful blankets. I snuggled in and held the receiver with both hands, as if afraid he'd slip away again.

"Hi!" I exclaimed. "How are you!? Are you OK?"

"I'm fine," he said with a chuckle.

"*Where* are you!?" I asked.

"I'm just a couple dimensions over," he said. His voice was soothing. "I'll be here for a little while."

We talked, and what I remember was the relief that he was not in pain. My breath came in gasps; the air in this wormhole was too precious. I knew it would not last. He finally said, "I gotta go, but I'm looking out for you."

I woke up feeling a peace and a lightness I hadn't felt for so long. I was sure I had really talked to him. I cried a little and went back to climbing the never-ending hill, but with a slightly lighter load. Maybe things might be OK one day?

The second: When my Gramma Mary Ann died, she had been suffering for so long I felt relief more than sadness. I knew I would miss her deeply, but we had nothing unresolved between us. We had never made it complicated. We loved each other—it was that simple.

One night, a few weeks after her death, I had a dream

where I woke in a large open field, sitting on a kitchen chair where two dirt roads crossed. The sun was shining, and the big white summer clouds smiled on. Next to me was a tiny wooden table with a gray Princess phone on it. It rang.

I picked it up and heard her joyful "Saaaaay! There's my girl!"

"Gramma!" I chimed. She sounded like she hadn't in years, her voice as ringing and robust as it used to be. "How are you?"

"Oh! I feel so much *better!*" she said. "I'm traveling and I feel great!"

The grass in the field pulsed greener. We talked a bit longer about this and that. I suddenly realized that this call would have to end. This might be my last chance.

"Gramma"—I choked up a little—"what do you have to tell me?"

She was quiet on the other end of the line for a second.

"Have your say," she said in a very sober and serious voice.

I told her I loved her, weeping in the dream.

She said, "I love you, too. I'll look out for you." Then: "OK, I gotta go! I need to get my connection to Thailand!" She sounded so pleased, and I was so happy that she was getting to travel again; that was something she had always loved. The joy was inflating and billowing across the sky.

"Bye, Gramma," I said.

"Bye, honey!" And she hung up the phone. The aftereffect of that dream lasted a long time, a month or so of me relaxing into my own confidence. I was bursting with gratitude. I knew she would never leave me.

The third: My friend Dallas Good's death in 2022 was a shock and a tragedy. No one was ready. But how can you be ready for someone to die? There was a tremor of grief across the continent like a rolling blackout. I could feel it disturbing my marrow. He was one of those people…a sort of generator for an entire region, for *so* many people. His influence was mighty.

In the weeks after, I hoped he would visit me in a dream. I needed answers.

One night I was awakened by summer desert smells, creosote and a sweetness.

The air was hot and thick, like silk panels billowing against your face. It was dark and I was indeed out in the Sonoran Desert. Dallas was there.

"There you are!"

"Hello, Neko," he said in his understated, affectionate way. He told me he was all right, good even!

"But, but…I'm so worried about Amanda," I cried. Amanda is Dallas's wife—they were the real thing, Dallas and Amanda, and over the past weeks, I'd worried for the grief she'd now be dragging with her.

"I've got her," he said matter-of-factly. "Don't worry anymore."

"OK." I choked back tears.

He smiled his huge, sunshine smile at me. Then that smile turned to something more mischievous. "Watch this," he instructed, then motioned at a dying, waist-high barrel cactus next to me. I somehow understood that he wanted me to pull apart the top of the cactus, where it was cracked open and rotting. As I did, he stepped his long, thin legs into it, up to his thighs. I stumbled back a step in awe. He tilted his head a little and grabbed the sides of the cactus and pulled it up around himself, thorns and all, like a pair of child's footie pajamas, chuckling and beaming.

"Oh my GOD! Is *that* what you can do on the other side!?" I laughed as he winked at me. Then the cactus suit, with him snug inside, began to descend into the earth like an elevator.

Chapter 24

The Most Tender Love

As a kid, I wanted nothing more than to be sitting on or near a horse. I remember quite clearly touching one as a baby. My Gramma Mary Ann was holding me and guiding my little baby hand to reach out to stroke the horse's brown shoulder. The horse breathed calmly as I touched it, and in that moment of contact it transferred its bottomless wonder to me. After that, all my memories are tinged with the knowledge that such creatures existed in the world. Of squinting my eyes and willing one to appear (and then making two). I wanted to ride one. I wanted to pet and brush one. I wanted to be one. I loved their strength and their beauty, their impossible lashes and root beer eyes.

"What is it with girls and horses?" people sometimes ask, often sounding on the edge of annoyance. I've been asked this for as long as I can remember, and never with any real curiosity.

They don't ask, "What's with boys and cars?" (or motorcycles, or speed or jumping off shit or playing army or...the list is endless). They also don't ask, "What's with girls and dolls?" (or girls and dresses). Horses are clearly too much for us to ask for. Even when horses were the number-one mode of transportation, it was taboo to ride as a woman unless you were very rich or very poor (nobody cared what you got up to then). There were fancy sidesaddles so you couldn't hang on properly. I'd love to know how many people were killed using those things. It was an issue even taken up by the suffragettes! Meanwhile, men were only worried about their daughters busting their hymens and no longer being virgins from riding astride. Their resale value would surely plummet.

The Victorians were such fascist prudes, they almost form a barrier against any history that comes before them. Sadly, their intense patriarchal era is what our society here in America is based on, and so as a group they're often difficult to circumvent. The ancient Greeks may have started it, but Queen Victoria, a fucking *woman*, really dug her heels in. She was a shame-based god-on-earth monarch. What does this have to do with horses? A lot.

When I was a kid there was always someone saying, "If you love horses so much why don't you marry one!?" (Gladly, shithook! Don't mind if I do!) It sounds like a harmless taunt, but there was always something strained and sinister underneath. In my young adulthood, the myth that Catherine the Great had sex with horses was the story that wouldn't go away, even though it had long ago been revealed as a vicious, prankish rumor started by a male detractor. And still, into adulthood, you'll hear people talk about the "erotic" nature of women's fascination with horses and power. Ugh, fuck off, Freud Jr., we don't want to fuck horses, we want to *be* horses. As simple as that. We want physical equality! We want to run free.

I think back to the horror comics I saw in my friend Penny Bowling's room—how the women on the covers looked flaccid (except for globe-ish breasts) and helpless, just captured, prone, and ready to be used. And then over the next couple of decades it was as if what was on those horror comic covers became real. The Green River Killer was on the TV and down the street. I felt my little bones growing into the curves of a cage, doubling back toward themselves, getting too close inside. Being a woman in this world means moving through constant threats of rape and predation, stalking and abuse. I've lived it, and I've seen it happen to *most* of the women I love.

Somewhere, early in my forties, it all seemed to catch up to me—the endless freight of being a woman. I was so depressed and beaten down, I just had to find the answer to the question that was gnawing at me: When in history did men start *hating* women and female-identifying people *so* much?

It's been *such* a long time, I had to visit *very* ancient history. I read many books; some made very good arguments for the breakdown and manipulation of egalitarian society in ancient Greece. Some talked about matriarchal and egalitarian societies all over Europe, Asia, and North America, now mostly extinct. I went to art school, where I was told that women had no freedoms so women couldn't possibly have made art or laws or plays or societies, even though they "may" have been capable. What a generous assessment! As a female-identifying person, I know my own tenacity and desire. I know the desires and passions of other women, and we are unstoppable. We have proven it time and time again down the millennia. We are not passengers, we are not drones. We are lightning and creation, so what I had learned and didn't learn never stopped my wondering. I knew we had *always* been here. I *felt* us. I *feel* us.

In my search through history, I found a great deal that made sense and other ideas that were just shallow graves and smoke screens. Women had been buried, but just barely. Societies all over the world think so little of women they haven't even made half an effort to cover over the evidence of our achievements. So *lazy*! They only did enough work to indict themselves later.

One magical day I came upon a book by a scholar named Adrienne Mayor called *The Amazons: Lives and Legends of Warrior Women Across the Ancient World*. With the help of other scholars and archaeologists, and the recent adoption of DNA evidence in scientific fields, Mayor essentially proves beyond a doubt the existence of egalitarian horse-warrior societies across Europe, Asia, and Northern Africa in which women were just as much at the forefront as the men were. They weren't man haters who cut off their own breasts; they were people using their brains and resources to survive. What made the women in these cultures different? Horses. They made us stronger and faster... and the Scythian recurve bow (and in some cultures, hunting eagles) made us some of the deadliest hunters and warriors the world has ever seen. We were here. Brightly, and on *fire*.

Horses were first tamed on the steppes north of the Black Sea around 4000 BCE. Women were just as involved as the men. Women tamed and held large herds, breeding them and using them for meat and milk as well as transportation and religious rites. The Amazon women were the first people to wear pants, which was looked down upon by the ancient Greeks. Women had freedom among the horses, and through our relationship to them we grew in intelligence, even having a little time to make art as well.

Horses do not respond cooperatively to aggressive commands. They are give-and-take beings. Sure, you can wrestle them into bondage and force them to do things through pain and fear, but that is no connection: That's cruelty. A horse's mind is not made to know the potential harm it can do to a human being. Otherwise, they would be about as tamable as a wild tiger. The average horse, weighing fifteen hundred pounds, could kill us accidently while trying to move a fly off its rear. A mere flinch is all it takes. I've been knocked to the ground standing next to one. But as a rule they would never do it on purpose. They are *re*active, which is their greatest gift to us if we choose to see it.

When I was a kid, I didn't have the worries of adults; my worries were large but different. I found it no trouble to connect with horses, just like I had no trouble connecting with cats or dogs. I was unafraid. Horses were different. Though they could hurt me, I knew it was only by way of my own negligence—being in the wrong place behind them or not anticipating their next move. Horses taught me to be hyperaware of my surroundings, and not under stress, but voluntarily and kindly, in a sensory way. I could bend for them like a little reed.

Horses do not lie. They do not manipulate. Their honesty leaves no room for you to doubt yourself. They tell you who they are and what they might be afraid of. Their light is like sun on a seed; your confidence grows and grows if you take the time to learn to listen to them. To stand next to a horse that accepts you and to touch its warm body and look into its gigantic, soft, kind eye is transporting. Your heart rate slows, and the endorphins release. There is no feeling like it; it is ancient and recalibrating.

I was forty when I got my first horse. When Norman came to live with me, he was really anxious. I was, too. It took us some false starts to get to know each other. I knew nothing of his history, as I had rescued him from a dealer/con man. It took a while to convince him I was a worthy leader of the herd, not just another person trying to trick or use him. I had a lot of help from my dear friend Heike, a master equestrian who is all about gentleness and freedom of choice for the horse. Out of necessity, I learned how to set my anxiety down for minutes at a time so that Norman would finally engage with me. It was so rewarding that I practiced and, as time went on, I was able to sustain it for longer and longer periods, feeling a calm, electric connection with him. This is why horses are often used as therapy animals for veterans, people with PTSD, and people who are nonverbal. Because horses don't lie, you know you've successfully put anxiety down for a minute when they give you their curious attention, or if they gently abide with you. They help you build that muscle that releases anxiety and develops your confidence. They help you find a little space to exhale, and maybe even let in a little joy.

My horses these days—I have two now—bring me a *lot* of joy. The trust we have built makes me feel so special, and their personalities have blossomed. Norm has even shed most of his anxiety, which I was able to help *him* achieve. He is so relaxed and so in love with his brother, Boon. They both welcome me enthusiastically, even when it's not feeding time. I have neighbors who come to just stand with them in the field and exhale as they put one hand on a giant, powerful shoulder. The horses make them feel safe. It breaks my heart and rebuilds it again.

We're related, the horses and I, and no one can tell me differently. We are old, old blood from back when women were free, just north of the Black Sea and beyond. This possibility of mutual respect and reciprocity is what little kids sense, I think: "I have a huge, strong, beautiful friend who *sees* me!" At least before they are taught to be competitive and treat horses like dirt bikes. I'm so thankful I was never exposed to that subculture, that it didn't have the chance to kill my ancient connection. My horses accept me as family, and I don't take it for granted. They even try to groom me with their teeth like I was one of them, but they never bite down; they know I am small and treat me tenderly. They are the friends and family I craved my whole life.

As much as I love them, I am not a horse, obviously. I am a person who is not quite a woman, not quite a man. I am what life has made me—someone who wishes to be gentle and is sometimes not. Someone with werewolf tufts who sometimes turns inside out. Perhaps this is true for you, too—a feeling of being a little bit strange, of having some fur and teeth, and shadows of the forest flickering across the back of your eyelids. If so, I wish you the exhalation of breath when your heart has synced with that of a horse, a friend, or another species, and that you can relax into a very real place, where you are the animal you were thousands of years ago, before people tried to wipe away your instincts with religion and greed and jealousy and fear. I wish you freedom and the knowledge of being a part of the world's tenderness. And I hope whenever the chance comes you will take it and feel your heartbeat along its true, original course—down the ever-changing river of you.

Acknowledgments

Colin Dickerman, Rachel Flotard, Carrie Frye, and Jen Gates; without the four of you this book would never have happened, thank you!

Jeff, Autumn and Susan Galegher. Bill Fortini and the entire Fortini family. Tara Challa, Brent and Jason Trople. All my bandmates past and present. Rickie Lee Jones, for writing such an inspiring memoir.

And YOU for coming to the show.

About the Author

Singer, songwriter, music producer, visual artist, and writer **Neko Case** has built a career with her distinctive style and musical versatility. In addition to her numerous critically acclaimed and Grammy-nominated solo records, Case is a founding member of the New Pornographers and has recorded a collaborative album with k.d. lang and Laura Veirs. She currently authors the popular biweekly Substack newsletter "Entering the Lung" and is writing the music for a high-profile Broadway production.